AIRDRIE

AIRDRIE

COMPILED BY
BOBBY ANDERSON
COPY EDITING BY HELEN HARRIS

ISBN: 9798320311746

Compiled and Edited by Bobby Anderson
Copy editing by Helen Harris
Cover by: Kirstie Piper
Cover Images by: Amy Hourigan (Color Photos), Bobby Duvall,
and Unknown

A Life in Ink:

Remembering Bobby Neil Anderson
(1926-2019)

Bobby Neil Anderson wasn't just a journalist; he was a storyteller who wore many hats throughout his remarkable 92 years. Born in Kentucky's Muhlenberg County, his love for narrative began early. Even while serving in the South Pacific with the US Army, he documented events for the Armed Forces paper.

Back in civilian life, his dedication to journalism blossomed. He carved a distinguished path in the industry - sports correspondent, editor, and even general manager. Under his leadership, the Milan Mirror, a Tennessee weekly, became a state leader. But his influence wasn't limited to print. His voice resonated on the airwaves as a radio sportscaster for the Times-Argus's affiliated station.

A man of unwavering dedication, Anderson balanced his journalism career with being a certified printer and a family man. He was also a songwriter and an author, forever etching his love for Muhlenberg County history in his book "Airdrie."

Bobby Neil Anderson's legacy extends far beyond the headlines he wrote. He leaves behind a cherished memory of a man whose passion for storytelling touched countless lives and communities.

Airdrie & Bobby Anderson

The Influence of Bobby's Work

When I first learned of the community of Airdrie and its mystique, I searched for a reliable source of information to learn more about the place. I found what I was looking for in Bobby Anderson's collection of stories and reminiscences about this once aspiring locale and the cooperative spirit and entrepreneurial efforts that surrounded its founding.

His compilation of writings and recollections is a one-stop treasure trove. It includes a 1908 detailed description by renowned Muhlenberg County historian Otto Rothert, as well as excerpts from Rothert's history of the county published in 1913.

Teachers, newspaper reporters, and many others share their stories and accounts in this compendium. Even the genealogies of those who lived and worked in Airdrie are woven into the book. Numerous photographs of the site, its abandoned ruins, and long-gone buildings fill the pages of Anderson's collection.

These recollections help keep alive the memories of the once-promising community on the banks of the Green River and shed light on what might have been.

- Michael Wortham

***

Many have asked the question of just whom was imprisoned at Airdrie Hill? The answer is straightforward, but it opens a complex tale of an American dream that originated in the wilderness of Muhlenberg County, Kentucky, in the 1850s.

When it comes to recounting such stories, few are more fitting than historian and author Bobby Anderson. Bobby, known for his hands-on approach, dug into records, conducted interviews with those possessing firsthand knowledge, and gathered some of the finest writings about Airdrie to write this book in 2001.

From his initial visit to Airdrie at the age of five, Bobby displayed a commitment to understanding the town and its residents. His comprehensive knowledge of this Scottish settlement, their attempted industry there and the local impact of Airdrie is explained in the in this writing.

- Barry Duvall

Forward

I am delighted that Lisa Piper is re-releasing Bobby Anderson's book, "AIRDRIE." If you are intrigued by and maybe tear up when you hear John Prine's song "Paradise," in which he talks about Muhlenberg County, Green River, Rochester, Paradise, and Airdrie Hill as well as Mr. Peabody's coal train, Bobby Anderson's book is a must read.

Airdrie has a special connection to my family. It is where my Great-Grandfather Archibald Pollock first settled after arriving in New York City on November 11, 1857 from Scotland with several of his siblings. Like many other immigrants the United States was the land of opportunity to him. As my great-great-grandfather said in a letter to an older son already in the United States, "A man cannot make a living here in Scotland."

Growing up, my Grandmother Margaret Ellen Penman Pollock, who was born just up the Green

River from Airdrie at Paradise, often told me stories about Airdrie. One of the often-told tales, true or not, was that Mammy Pollock worked as a teenager for General Don Carlos Buell.

I visited Airdrie several times as a young boy with my father, Archie D. Pollock, and was in awe of the workmanship of the furnace, stone house, and steps. Each time I visited, my imagination ran rampant as I visualized my ancestors being there.

While a failure as an iron producer, Airdrie lives today in the hearts and minds of my family and the ancestors of the men and women who first settled there. To us, Airdrie was the opening door to the land of opportunity.

-Archie D. Pollock, Jr.

Two views of Airdrie,
its stack and stone
house, possibly
before 1900.

—Photo courtesy of
Gelnn and Anna
Johnson

Table of Contents

OLD AIRDRIE:

Preface

I first saw Old Airdrie when I was five. That would have been in 1931. I was taken there for a family picnic by my father and mother and my father's cousin, Leonard Anderson and his family. It was Leonard Anderson who first imparted to me tidbits of the interesting history of Muhlenberg County. He also loaned me his personal copy of Otto Rothert's *History of Muhlenberg County* when I was ten. I called him "Cousin Leonard" at that time. Later, when he was my grade school teacher, "Cousin Leonard" sounded a little too sissy for me. So I called him "Leonard". But only once. After that, I respectfully referred to him as "Mr. Anderson". I found that he could be just as stern as I also knew him to be lovable and kind.

Some folks called it Airdrie Hill. Others Old Airdrie. Most couldn't, didn't, or wouldn't call it Air-Drie. They pronounced it A-Drie — with a long "A". I also did. I did not learn differently for many years.

At that first sighting of Airdrie, I became a fan. I saw first only the tumbled down remnants of a house or two cowering in an overgrown field. Where once town streets were laid out to accommodate hotels, lathed and plastered homes, stores and other small businesses which proudly stood on Airdrie Hill in the 1850s, now only these remnants of an old house or two seemed to try to "hunker down" behind scrub oak and sedge grass to hide in shame their run-down conditions.

I thrilled at the long flight of stone steps leading from the top of Airdrie Hill, down the bluff and toward the furnace and Green River. I counted them going down. I counted them coming back up. I just as quickly forgot how many I had counted.

In later visits, I noted one step was missing. Perhaps pushed off the flight to its "death" many feet below by pranksters or vandals. This left a gap in the flight of steps not unlike the gap where a seven-year-old's front tooth is missing. I counted the steps up and I counted them down again, time after time, on each succeeding visit and promptly forgot each time how many steps there were.

I marveled at the stone work of the old furnace and the machine shop. I listened patiently as the now-debunked old tales were told of how a slave jumped to his death from the top of the bluff into the gaping mouth of the fiery furnace. Or another — the same facts, but this time a state prisoner who took his only life in the same manner. It is best to be known now that no slave labor and no state prisoners were ever used in the construction of the Airdrie facility or in its brief operation. Interesting tales, nonetheless.

Either of those men cited in these stories would have been a great athlete. It would have had to have been the longest, most accurate broad jump in the history of the Olympics.

I have crawled and crept into the mouth of the nearby opening in the hillside, purported to be the original *"McLean Old Bank"*, Muhlenberg's first commercial coal mine. I can't even vouch for the veracity of that tale. It was, indeed, one opening. It may or may not have been McLean's original.

I have drunk many times from the old spring a few steps from the river bank at Airdrie. I don't know why. The water is not good. It is filled with sulphur and other minerals giving it a foul, putrid taste, leaving its bitterness in one's mouth for a long, long time. Still, I went back to drink time after time. It was as if some magnet would draw one to its edge to partake of its offering. Like you had no choice. You must drink. Then you would wish you hadn't.

It has been many years since I have been to Airdrie. Over those years, I have collected the writing of other authors including Mr. Rothert, Agnes Harralson, reporters from the Evansville, Louisville and Owensboro newspapers, and from various historic publications and books. In the pages which follow, I have assembled all of these in this one booklet so that the reader might have all of them in total. Some of the stories seem a little far-fetched in content. Some of the contents given as facts are obviously false or fiction — yet, in each case, I have included their writings, verbatim, so that the reader might have the full scope of what others have had to say about Old Airdrie.

As a child, I instantly became a fan of Old Airdrie. I still am.

I wonder how long it will take the county, the state or federal agencies to become fans. This is a historic effort crying out for preservation. Old Airdrie has stood of its own strength for many, many years. Now it deserves the aid of someone to insure its preservation for the eons of future generations. Who will step forward?

(Bobby Anderson)

Annals of Airdrie
in Five Chapters
By OTTO A. ROTHERT
Reprinted from the Greenville (Ky.) Record, 1908

Chapter I
A Trip to the Town of Tradition

The other day while on Main Street viewing Greenville's new courthouse and admiring its imposing steps, its six massive Corinthian columns, its solid brick walls and stone trimmings, its towering dome and its striking clock, I was only doing what every visitor and citizen of Greenville has done again and again since that beautiful building was completed last year. The structure certainly is worthy of the admiration so lavishly bestowed upon it. But while looking on this new courthouse, I could still see, with my mind's eyes, the old courthouse that stood on the same grounds for more than sixty years. Watching the removal of the old landmark was like the bidding of a last farewell to a long time friend. The old house had years before outlived the spirit of progress of the county, so when its long postponed day of doom finally came, the same eye that dropped a tear of sorrow while the old bricks were being torn down, likewise shed a tear of joy while the new walls were going up.

While thus standing on the new concrete walk and leaning against an iron awning post meditating over all the many changes caused by the development of the county's mineral and agricultural resources, my friend, Joe H. Bohannon gently saluted me with a small book he held in his hand and aroused me from my reverie. We commented on the graceful piece of architecture before us and on the evident fact that many of the old Muhlenberg landmarks are rapidly passing away to make room for the present day demands.

This brought up the subject of old Airdrie on Green River, in this county, whose historical ruins will soon disappear, for on their original site, new buildings and mining sheds, it is said, are to be erected in the near future. We had, some weeks previous, decided to make a final visit to Airdrie this fall. He called my attention to the fact that that season had now come, for its arrival was not only shown by the calendar but nature itself revealed its presence everywhere. Joe Bohannon then opened his pamphlet with which he had a few moments before greeted me. It contained some of the recently published poems of Clarence B. Hays, the James Whitcomb Riley of the Green River country, one of Greenville's brightest sons, who died last February at the age of thirty. I here quote in full his *"Then Fall Comes Rollin' 'Round."*

> When the rabbit's jest begun to hop,
> An' you've finished harvestin' yer crop,
> An' the hickory nuts begin to drop,
>   An' clatter to the ground;
> When the nights air long an' gettin' cold,
> `An' leaves have turned from green to gold,
> An' yer sheep's a-blatin' in the fold,
>   Then Fall comes rollin' 'round.

When the mornin's cool and powerful still,
An' the sage grass yaller on the hill,
An' you've took yer wheat crop to the mill,
　　An' paid to have it ground;
When yer hate's to quit yer mornin' doze,
When the frost's a-bitin' on yer toes,
An' yer ain't bought no winter clothes,
　　Then Fall comes rollin' 'round.

When they've started up the dee-strict school,
An' the blue bird feels it gettin' cool,
An' starts, accordin' to its rule,
　　To Southern eatin' ground;
When the punkin's yaller on the vine,
An' yer likes to fool away yer time,
A-layin' 'round in warm sunshine,
　　Then Fall comes rollin' 'round.

When yer tobacker's cut an' in the barn,
An' yer wife's a-spinnin' winter yarn,
You've patched the fences 'round the farm,
　　An' seed wheat is in the ground;
When you've worked all year an' done yer best,
A fixin' up yer winter nest,
Yer always ready fer a rest,
　　When Fall comes rollin' 'round.

The appointed season, so interestingly portrayed in
this poem, having evidently arrived, we concluded to
begin our contemplated pilgrimage the next day to old
Airdrie.

3

Nothing authentic, as far as we knew, had ever been published on the history of this "Deserted Village." We were aware that a few absurd tales and ghost stories had crept into print, but like last year's almanac, they have performed the service for which they were intended and are now no more.

Some of the space writers who devoted many columns to the subject, I judge have never seen the place. One described it as being located in Green County; another in Ohio County; and another placed it near Evansville, Indiana.

We were told that a mineralogical report on the Airdrie furnace and property had been published in 1884 in a work by the Kentucky Geological Survey, entitled *"Western Coal Fields,"* the same being a reprint of an original report made in 1874 by P. N. Moore to Professor N. S. Shaler in charge of the survey.

We had no desire to read this groundless fiction on the subject and the printed geological report not being available at the time, we decided to gather as many facts and dates pertaining to Airdrie as possible from among old citizens.

We devoted half a day in Greenville to interviewing a number of people. The next morning we drove to Drakesboro and spent the night with the genial J. C. Haden, after which we proceeded to Paradise on Green River. From Paradise we wandered to Airdrie, located one mile further down the river.

After a few hours on this historic hill and around the old stone walls, we retraced our steps to Paradise. We next drove to Central City for the purpose of seeing some of our friends in that place and having an interview with them relative, of course, to the traditions of Airdrie. After a night in South Carrollton, we returned to Greenville.

We consulted all the old men and women we found along the highways and byways. We entered every smoking barn in sight to interview those in charge of firing their tobacco. We opened many a gate and "rested our hats" on many a front porch. On one occasion we leisurely climbed a rail fence, but a moment later we jumped over the same rails back on the Big Road — just to show that our four legs could run faster than those of the approaching "brute cow."

While we acknowledge we may not have gathered many facts during this expedition, pertaining to Airdrie, we must confess we experienced more than a little fun. But since our personal experience will be of no interest to you, I will try to confine our account to what we regard as reliable data bearing directly on the case and omit all statements we feel are based on groundless rumors, except in one instance which I shall try to quote verbatim.

But unfortunately, these facts are, for the greater part, very little more than names and dates. While at Airdrie our eyes feasted on a very romantic scene, but the romantic tales that reached our ears were very few in proportion. So, at the risk of being extremely dry and tedious, I now record much of what we heard. If the patient reader, after perusing this first chapter is not convinced that this written account is "dry and tedious", he will be before he finishes what follows. However we publish it with the hope that our efforts will, in a printed form, help, not only to perpetuate the many scattered verbal records now passing from sire to son, but will also aid each man to connect his own legend to those told by others. We found that most of the people whom we consulted were familiar with their own ancestors' connection with Airdrie but were unfamiliar with its history previous to or after their kinsman's particular time.

One of our informers, the exceptional character referred to above was a man of many wandering words but little knowledge on the subject of Airdrie. He met us along the Big Road while we were watering our horses. To our questions as to what he knew about Airdrie and how the town of Paradise received its name, he answered:

"So that's what you're drivin' at! When I see you get out of that rig says I to myself, them can't be drummers, for drummers darn seldom waters their stock, and them can't be preachers, for preachers generally always has black coats on. I knowed you wasn' dox (doctors), fur dox never wear them yeller cookoo pants. But I reckon since you are lookin' after the dead and not the livin', you must be undertakers or tombstone agents.

"But you axt me why that town was called Paradise. When you get there you'll see no earthly reason why the place is called Paradise. There may be a *bibolical* (sic) reason; I can't say, for I ain't no parson. And don't know nothing about geology. It might be some squatter hit the place in a way back times and thought he was clean off this world and so he might 'ave allowed he had struck Paradise or some other place then and there. Or, he might have been a tie cutter, fur in olden times, even when I was a young one, this whole county was full of the finest trees you ever laid your eyes on, so a tie hacker would most sure have called it Paradise.

"If my gran'pa was alive he could tell a heap about old times and Granny could have told you a right smart too. But they've jined the silent majority. A-dry (Airdrie) sure belongs to be writ up while the scribers still have a chance to jog the memory of the old timers. Now, naming the old timers, that makes me recollect a thing or two. Gran'pa used to say that when his pa came here the Stom boys run a one-horse store at Paradise. They got all their goods by boat and being there are always so little to unload for them, the deck roustabouts was always glad when they landed at Stom's landin'. They said to theirselves, 'this place is a picnic.' So, according to that line of arguing, had Stom's landin' been born in our day the place just as like as not, might have been called Picnic.

"But I've got an idea that that ain't just exackly the whys and wherefores of that name. I've some time or other heard it said how she was named, but I reckon I've just clear forgot. All I can say for sure is that some man named her. There is no need of axing when you get to Paradise, for there is no living man on that bluff old enough to tell.

"But you say what do I know about A-dry? Well sir, I been living in these parts fur ten years, off and on, and ain't been there but onct. I was bornd in Missouri, raised and schooled in the swamps of Arkansas, married in Tennessee and then came to Old Kaintuck. My Lordy, but Arkansas is a mighty sorry country. My next move was to Illinois, where I was skinned and kicked out of house and home by some stock — not livestock, but some dead mining stock operatin' somewhere in New Mexico. And here I am on my way to Central to see Robinson's Big Tent Show Combined.

"I ain't much on dead towns like A-dry. But I sure would be proud to carry you two gents and your rig over there. I got some friends in business in Central, down there by the depot. But what I aimed to tell you was about the time I went to A-dry. I happened along the day the General had a threshing machine outfit there. This was in the summer of 1898. You see, the old General never did any farming. The nighest he ever came to it was raisin' a little garden stuff and a watermelon patch. Now, most men guard their patches with a shotgun, but the old gent watched hisen with field glasses.

"This particular year he raised a crop of oats just for the fun of having it thrashed. It turned out eighty bushels by measurement, and the lord only known how much less by weight. Anyhow, I was there. He invited everybody and they all came from far and near, and and it looked like he had more eaters than he and Carter had bushels of oats. He said it was his first, last and only thresher dinner and he wanted to do her up right. I ain't seed nothing like it before it nor since. There was dozens of this, gallons of that and bushels of t'other. The tables was loaded to fare-you-well and you can believe me or not, they had to brace it up with some dimension timbers to keep it from breaking or sagging to the floor. I heard one man say the table fairly groaned, but I'm most sure I never heard it, for I was busy making the feed perish.

"I knowed the thesher outfit and the company would hike out before sundown and leave over half the grub. So I hung around that night and the next morning they gave me enough to run me and my kinfolks fur a month of Sundays.

8

"When I was marching over the hill with my tub full of cooked grub, I met up with a feller sashaying around some old buildings that them Scotch lived in years back. He looked hungry — this feller did — and as "When I was marching over the hill with my tub full of cooked grub, I met up with a feller sashaying around some old buildings that them Scotch lived in years back. He looked hungry — this feller did — and as hanted as some of the dead houses, so I told him he could eat out of my tub and then go down to the General's and he would fill him up to the neck with more fine grub. He was polite like and said he had done dined. One word unkivered another. I told him I was a cropper and he said to me he was one of these poets what writes poetry. He looked all skin and bones and puney, so I thought I might encourage the feller by asking him to turn some poetry loose on me. He gave me what, if I recollect right, he called a Blacksmith's Parable on the Demolished and Abolished Village. No, I'll take that back; he named it a something else on a Deserted Village. It started like this:

Old A-dry, historical village of the hills,
Where the Scotlanders worked the deep boring drills;

"In another place it went this fashion:
And still they gazed and wondered more than enough;
That one big bluff could hold such very fine stuff.

"I knowed if I set around with him much longer the hogs would get in my tub and I'd catch it from the old woman when I landed to home. He grabbed my mitt in his two fists and says he: 'A due, a due, kind friend a due.' I told him I was due home last night, but he could do as he pleased about staying.

"That was the first and last I saw of that duck, but I have a kind of an idea he is down in Hopkinsville now."

We bade our roadside friend adieu. A few hours afterwards upon our arrival at Paradise, we learned that while some of our late companion's statements may have been groundless, the one based on the oats threshing was verified by many other men, both old and young.

* * *

Chapter II
Airdrie as Seen Today

Upon our arrival at old Airdrie, we found the place greatly changed since our last visit some five years previous. All the houses built by Alexander had disappeared, except two, one of which standing on the original town site, is now occupied by the widow Wheeler, and the other, known as the Half Way House, located half way between the old furnace and Paradise, is at present occupied by Nat Huckleberry. Some of the old houses have been carried away in the shape of lumber to various parts of the county, while the others that fell down years ago are today a pile of decaying wood.

The Buell residence was not only the oldest house in the now demolished village but was also the largest and most comfortable, and up to the last the best preserved of them all. The spacious old house was unfortunately destroyed by fire two years ago. Nothing now remains of the famous old dwelling except two stone chimneys, the old stone foundation and the walls of a stone milkhouse. We found

10

the riverbank park, so beautifully kept for many years, now almost a jungle, with its winding paths rampant with ivy and honeysuckle, its foot bridges broken and tottering and its tree-shaded lawn overgrown with wild weeds and bushes and run-wild shrubbery and vines. But the landscape, seen from the village hill, showing Green River in the foreground, with the fertile farms and the green forests on the opposite shore, is as attractive as ever.

We walked down from the top of the hill on which the village once stood to the long narrow strip of land lying between the hill and the river. Among some of the wild cedars and sycamores we discovered a tall brick chimney and near it two rusty boilers. Here and there, protruding above the grass, we noticed traces of the old stone walls that reminded us more of some work of prehistoric mound builders than a foundation made last century by mill builders. Two of the old shafts we chanced to see looked like long abandoned wells and another like a mere swag in the ground. We also passed a few cave-like entrances leading into the side of the hill from which, evidently, coal had, at one time, been taken.

The old furnace still stands as majestically as ever. Its upper half is an iron cylinder-shaped shell, enclosing a cylinder-shaped stone wall about 30 feet high and 20 feet in diameter, resting upon a stone base about 25 feet square and 20 feet high, giving the furnace a total height of about 50 feet.

Near the stack is the Stone House, whose massive walls seem able to defy storm and sunshine for many centuries yet to come. It is a sand stone structure, fifty by twenty feet, three stories high. The wooden doors and window frames have long ago fallen away. This fort-like mass was at one time covered with slate which, unfortunately, was ruined by visitors throwing rocks on it from the top of the hill near the foot of which the house is located.

The shingle roof, placed on it when the house was prepared for state prisoners, has since met the same fate as the original slate. About half way up the front wall of this structure, between two of the windows, the thoughtful masons placed a large stone bearing the prominent inscription:

AIRDRIE
1855.

The famous hillside Stone Steps, leading from a point just beyond the Stone House to the top of the hill, is even more picturesque than ever. Virginia Creeper has found its way further up the solid stone foundation and the drooping branches of the nearby trees are now sheltering clusters of clinging fern and moss. The sixty narrow stone steps, although without bannister or handrail, can be climbed in safety by any sober man, and in ecstasy by any two lovers.

The Stack, the Stone House, and the Stone Steps, all weather-beaten, with the tall young trees around them, when viewed together from a short distance suggest a bygone day and time with which our imagination could associate any long-past years of the world's history, did not the deep chiseled figures of *"1855"* keep our mind from wandering back any further.

Airdrie of today is indeed a romantic looking spot. Although few visitors know its history, all of them nevertheless enjoy gazing at its forlorn and ancient looking walks, standing so solemnly on the banks of this deep and beautiful river. Even the most prosaic spectators will experience a sense of reverence and mystery creep over them at the site of Airdrie's three abandoned and time-worn stone structures.

* * *

Chapter III
The Pre-Airdriean Days

Airdrie is about one mile below Paradise. Paradise, the older of the two, is located on land originally settled by Jake and Henry Stum (or Stom), who began to establish themselves on Green River during the latter part of the 18th century. They conducted a small store in association with their farm. Their boat landing was for many years known as Stum's Landing and it is very likely that before their deaths, along in the 1840s, the name of the settlement was changed to Paradise.

Jake Stum is said to have been "long, lean and lanky", weighing only 70 pounds and measuring about six feet in height. He was never known to be sick but once. On that one occasion while confined to his bed room with "the slow fever", a new doctor, who was unacquainted in the neighborhood, was summoned. The physician had never seen Jake "stand on his pegs", so tradition says , nor had he ever heard of his feathery weight. So when he stepped into Jake's room he asked to be shown the sick man. At the sight of the "skin and bones" the frightened doctor rushed out of the house saying Jake was even less mortal than a living skeleton. He informed the family that Jake, although "able to sit up and eat a snack", must have died some months ago, but owing to the absence of flesh the worms made no attack on him, and it was just his spirit that talked through the skin and bones. Jake recovered from that attack of typhoid fever and lived many years after.

His brother Henry, on the other hand, was a man of normal proportions but never enjoyed the best of health. Both were upright and highly respected men and lived to a ripe old age.

In 1802 when Peter Scholl came to Paradise from Pennsylvania, he found no one located in the immediate vicinity except the Stum families. Peter's father served seven years in the Revolution; Peter himself served two years in the War of 1812 and Peter's son, E. C. Scholl, served four years in the Civil War, making a total of thirteen years of active military service in three generations of the Scholls.

The next influential man to appear on the scene at Paradise was George W. Haden, the father of Joe C. Haden. George W. Haden was born in Maryland in 1813. He was the son of Joseph Haden, a pioneer of Kentucky, who at the time of the birth of his son was temporarily located in Hagerstown, Maryland. His parents made the return trip west over the mountain on their return to Kentucky on horseback, carrying their little son George with them. George W. Haden's mill was the first saw mill erected in the vicinity of Paradise. After running a horse power, "upright saw" or "sash saw" a few years, he introduced a circular saw run by steam, the first of its kind in the county[1]. His mill business was well established when Alexander began building Airdrie. He sawed all the lumber used in the erection of its houses. He also built the flat boats used by the various coal operators who mined at Airdrie before the arrival of Alexander.

George W. Haden was one of the best known men of his day. He was a staunch supporter of the South. After the breaking out of the Civil War he was too far advanced in years to enter the army. However, he patriotically presented his fighting brethren with much stock and other food. When General Buckner passed through Greenville with his army on his way to Ft. Donelson, the General expressed a great admiration of a sorrel horse the old

---

[1] Actually, the first steam powered sawmill in Muhlenberg County was operated by Edward Weir on Caney Creek in 1848, followed by Mr. Haden's Mill.

gentleman was riding in the town at the time, and offered to buy him. "Reindeer" was the pride of the family and the owner therefore did not feel at liberty to give or sell the animal to anyone. Upon his return to his home near (present-day) Drakesboro, he informed his wife, "Aunt Lucy", of General Buckner's desire to own their bay. She immediately sent the horse back to Greenville and presented him to the General with her compliments. The same animal was shot from under General Buckner at Ft. Donelson on February 15, 1862.

Airdrie as said is about one mile from Paradise. The land on which the town was later built was patented in 1810 by William McLean, who in the early 1830s built the residence later known as the Buell House

William McLean was the oldest son of Judge Alney McLean who organized a company in this locality and, as their captain, fought with them through the war of 1812. The five sons of Judge Alney McLean were William, who died in 1870 and, as just stated, was the first owner of the Airdrie place. Charles and Alney Jr. were twins. They lived in this county all their lives and were well-known farmers and merchants. Charles died about 1893 and Alney about 1903, both having reached a very old age. It was the Charles McLean who, in 1840, while living at Airdrie, was admitted to West Point Military Academy. His dislike for military discipline, combined with his longing to be at home with his twin brother Alney, resulted in his leaving West Point shortly after entering it. Simon Bolivar Buckner, then a boy of 17, employed as a clerk at the Buckner Furnace, at that time owned by his father, was appointed a cadet to succeed Charles McLean. S. B. Buckner graduated from the Academy in July, 1844 and, as is well known, was immediately promoted by the army.

Judge Alney McLean's fourth son, Sam, spent most of his years in the South. Robert, the youngest boy, lived in Granada, Mississippi, where he became an eminent lawyer.

Besides these five sons, Judge Alney McLean had four daughters: Eliza, who married Mr. McBride of Canton, Mississippi; Transalvania (sic), who after the death of Eliza, married her sister's husband; Tabitha and Roena, who lived and died in Greenville but were never married.

William McLean, builder of the Buell House, was the first to occupy the house and also the first man to mine coal around Airdrie. After the death of his father he removed his mother and her children to Greenville to his new quarters. While the McLean family was living there, William was married. William and his bride lived at Airdrie a few years and drifted into the south but frequently returned to visit the house he had built.

In those days steamboats plied the Green River between Bowling Green and Louisville. None ever passed the McLean house without a salute, for it was from far and near that point many of his Greenville people took passage. About the year 1844 what was then the newest and finest boat on Green River was named *"Lucy Wing"* in honor of the daughter of Charles Fox Wing, now Mrs. W. H. Yost, whose beauty, like that of her sister's, was far famed. Captain Culver was always in charge of the *"Lucy Wing"*. He was a great reader and made it a point to have all his passengers read *"Poems by Amelia"*, a popular publication of 1845.

William Duncan, of Bedford, Indiana, was the next man to work on the mine after McLean left. He, however, did not occupy the house. He was represented by his son-in-law, J. W. Newlan. Duncan Place, on the *Illinois Central*, now known as Nelson Station, was so named in honor of his family.

16

Thomas Carson, of Bowling Green, representing Hinds & Carson, who worked the mine for a few years, was the second man to occupy the house, and very likely, the last preceding the arrival of Alexander.

We attempted to give you an idea as to how old Airdrie looks today and also referred to some of the old citizens who lived in and around Airdrie and Paradise previous to Alexander's time. We shall next try to tell in what way Alexander, Buell and others were connected to his historic spot.

* * *

Chapter IV
The Reign of Alexander

Airdrie derives its name from a small city of the same name in Scotland, located between Edinburgh and Glasgow. It is the old home of the titled Alexanders. Robert Aitcheson Alexander, the founder of Airdrie in Muhlenberg County, was born in Frankfort, Kentucky, in 1819. He was the son of the Honorable Robert Alexander and the grandson of Sir William Alexander and his wife, who was a Miss Aitcheson of the House of Airdrie, Scotland. Robert's oldest brother was a bachelor and was named, like their father, Sir William. This William, the bachelor, promised his brother Robert, then living in the bluegrass region of Kentucky, to educate his oldest son, Robert Aitcheson, and to let him succeed to his title and estate if he would send him over to Scotland for that purpose.

This was done and after Sir William's death, Robert Aitcheson Alexander fell heir to the estate. Some years after the death of his uncle he decided to return to America in order to be near his brother and sisters: Alexander John Alexander, Mrs. J. B. Waller and Mrs. H. C. Deeds. Besides his supply of Black Band ore in Scotland was about exhausted. He made a search for the same ore in

America. Through his geologist, Alexander Hendrie, he discovered its existence near Paradise about 1850. This discovery was verified by another of his geologists, James Gilmore, who came over from Scotland in 1852. Thus encouraged with these discoveries in his own native state, Alexander bought about 17,000 acres of land, all of which with the exception of the Buckner Furnace lay around Paradise.

Alexander believed the Scotch were the most competent iron workers and so he brought many of his former employees and their families to his new Airdrie. A special ship was chartered for the trip. It required six weeks for their sailing vessel to cross the ocean. Tradition says they had a collision with "a water logged sailing vessel" which threw them out of their course to such an extent they landed in New York instead of Philadelphia.

The name of Alexander's special chartered ship seems to have been lost by the preservers of Airdrie's tradition. However one enthusiast suggested that since the Pilgrim Fathers came over on the *Mayflower*, it might be chronologically, if not logically, concluded that these Sons of Scotland followed later on the *June Bug*.

Travelling to Pittsburgh they came down the Ohio River and after some delay in Louisville started up the Green in small steamboats. One of the lady passengers, while going up the Green River one night, remarked to some of her companions that she was surprised to see the new country so thickly populated. She judged that ever light she saw came from a house, but she soon discovered that houses were few and far between and lightning bugs were numerous.

Upon their arrival at their "*New Scotland*" they immediately set to work building the town of Airdrie. Thus in 1854 was started that Scotland colony most of whose members remained in the country or vicinity and who are today represented by their many descendants. Gilbert V. Glenn, a son of Moses F. Glenn, a member of the Alney McLean company in the War of 1812, was among the few natives who helped the carpenters immediately after their arrival. Other natives were employed later on.

The plans for the Stone House and Furnace were drawn by John Hendrie in Scotland who, however, did not see these structures until sometime after they were abandoned. He made three trips to America, the last extending from the fall of 1904 to 1906, during which time he lived in the Buell House. He now resides in Scotland and when last heard from was still alive.

William Torrents was their engine builder, in which capacity he had also worked in Scotland. He later served as general manager of the works. After the place was abandoned he farmed across the river from Airdrie and them removed to Rockport where he died.

Robert Kipling, the pattern maker, was the only Englishman who came with the crowd. He, too, later drifted into farming and died in this vicinity in 1903. Kipling, like every other man in Airdrie, was an admirer of James Jackson Robertson, one of the well-known characters from the Upper Pond Creek country. Kipling cast a number of door props called "Old Jack Robertson." They were small iron figures about 10 inches long and five inches high, showing "Old Jack" sitting on the floor with his legs stretched out, a goose between them, and he in the act of carving it. The head is hollow and works on a hinge. A few of these iron door weights can still be found in Muhlenberg County.

Robert Patterson, another of the Scotch party, was the book keeper and one of the civil engineers. It was he who surveyed a line from Airdrie while in operation, to the old Buckner Stack, which had been abandoned some fifteen years before.

Gilbert Muir and William Williamson were also of the Scotch colony. Muir retained charge of the machinery long after the place was abandoned. He moved to Ohio County where he lived to an old age. William Williamson was a young man in those days and has since spent most of his time around the mines and is now an overseer in one of William G. Duncan's large mines in this county.

Two Scotchmen by the names of Toll and Macdougal, whose descendants still live in this county, were among those originally identified with Airdrie.

William Murray was, as far as we could learn, the only man who met an accidental death around Airdrie during Alexander's time. While crossing a walk log over a slough between Airdrie and Paradise, he slipped and fell into the water. His hat was discovered floating on the surface which led to the finding of his body. He was buried in the Dearing Burying Ground about one mile west of Airdrie. Another man is said to have drowned in the same place and under different circumstances. If such is the case, tradition seems to have lost his name.

Most of the Scotlanders who were brought to this country by Alexander were Presbyterians. Although they had no church building, they did not neglect their religion but met every Sunday morning at one of the homes.

None of the people we interviewed could recall having heard of any incident connected with any weddings during Alexander's reign. However, they all agreed that some of the slaves "jumped the broomstick" and thus became "man and wife."

Amusements of all sorts were on their programs. They were good fishermen and splendid swimmers but paid little attention to hunting and trapping. Archie Pollock, another member of the original colony, was the champion fist fighter or pugilist. In fact, it is said that friendly fist fights were indulged in more than any other sport. Dances were frequently given. Jarret Wallace was their fiddler. Traces of Scotch airs introduced by him can still be heard at some of the "old fiddlers contests" given in this county. "Uncle Jarret" died near Paradise in 1870. Robert T. Wallace of Greenville is one of his grandsons.

One version of tradition says that Scotch high balls and Kentucky toddies would occasionally disturb the tranquillity of the town. Laley's Brewery was established near Paradise on Green River during Alexander's day. Both "corn juice" and "barley beer," it is said, were made there up to shortly before the Civil War. While Laley's place may have been known as a "still house" we rather suspect that during the after-working-hours visits of the Airdrietes, it was temporarily converted into a "rough house." But in spite of their occasional nocturnal trips to the "still house" the furnace men would always be found at their posts of duty "on Green River, without a headache", the next morning.

Alexander Hendrie, or "Scotch Henry", and James and Mathew Gilmour as said, were Alexander's geologists. After Airdrie was abandoned by Alexander, "Scotch Henry" located on the Bucker Furnace tract where he farmed a number of years. Even during his residence at Airdrie, he made many trips to this tract of land on Upper Pond Creek, for it was at that time owned by Alexander. Tradition says "Scotch Henry" rode a vicious bay mare, always using two bits. He frequently found it necessary to apply the "emergency bit" while dashing like a deer through the woods between the two places — some fifteen miles. He fell heir to an estate in Scotland, to which country he returned and remained until 1864 at the age of 54. His wife survived him by a number of years and both are now buried in Ohio County.

In 1874, Alexander Hendrie sent his oldest son, Charles, to a mining school in Scotland. Charles remained until

21

1875 when he married and returned to Kentucky. He is now manager and mining engineer for Drakesboro Coal & Mining Company at Drakesboro.

James Gilmour (Gilmore), who died near Airdrie in 1895, was the father of James. G. Gilmour now of Paradise. We succeeded in finding only one of Gilmour's records. I will here refer to it, not so much to call attention to the richness of the strata at Airdrie, as to show the accuracy of his work and depth of his drillings, for his statement has been verified by a number of investigations made since 1857, and under better conditions.

The shaft in question was sunk to a depth of 483 feet for the purpose of finding another band of ore. In the bottom of this shaft a drill hole was put down 320 feet where a fine grade of Black Band ore was discovered. This is very likely the same vein of iron ore worked at the Buckner Furnace some fifteen years before. Of the coal veins ranging from No. 12 on down, 36 feet was reported by Gilmour as workable. No. 5, found at the bottom of the shaft, was said to be the finest coal and above it was found an eight foot stratum of iron balls. Interspersed between the veins of coal are many fine strata of fine fire clay. In fact, Alexander made his own brick out of clay dug in the immediate neighborhood of the village.

Alexander spared no expense in any of his work. The capital at his disposal for the undertaking seemed unlimited. It is said he invested over $350,000 "and then walked right away from it."

He enlarged the Buell House and retained a few rooms in it for his personal use. He built a large two-story frame hotel, a store building, a few two-story dwellings and about thirty cottages consisting of two rooms, a hall and a kitchen. Each of these houses was lathed and plastered and supplied with a massive chimney and large open fireplaces.

Everybody, regardless of his position around the works, was comfortably located.

After considerable drilling, digging and delaying, the furnace was finally started. Alexander, as said before, believed the Scotch were the most competent iron workers in the world and he therefore gave them full sway. While his men may have been thoroughly familiar with the handling of the Black Band iron ore of Scotland, they evidently did not realize that the ore here required a different treatment. Three or four unsuccessful attempts were made to run the furnace. The trouble lay not in the ore but in its management. Had they changed some of the managers and with them some of their methods, the undertaking would have been a grand success.

Alexander's patience soon gave out.. He cared very little about the money involved for it was only a small percent of his fortune. He set a date for the discontinuing of the work, and although the drillers discovered more iron ore on the pre-announced day, Alexander nevertheless clung to his firm resolution and discontinued the work. This was in the fall of 1857. He retired to his stock farm near Lexington, where, it is said, he did more than any other man toward the improvement of blooded stock in the state. At the time of his death on his farm in 1870 he was reputed to be the richest man in Kentucky.

Sir Robert Aitcheson Alexander was a bachelor. Although he had a title, he was seldom addressed by it in this country. He was a quiet, modest, unassuming man. His employees called him "*Lord*". On one occasion a backwoodsman by the name of Williams paid a visit to Airdrie and upon his arrival immediately asked for "that there *Lord*." Alexander was pointed out to him. Williams, it is said, "sashayed around him and sized him up from head to foot" and then expressed his astonishment by saying: "So you are a *Lord*, are you? By gum, you are nothin' but a human bein' after all, and a plain, ordinary, say-little sort of a feller at that. They said you was a Big Bug, but five foot six will reach you any day of the week, by Washington." This amused Alexander for he realized how unconsciously but truthfully the speaker described him. He gave Williams a hearty handshake and a few weeks later, the backwoodsman presented "*Lord Elick*" with "enough venison for all Scotland."

* * *

Chapter V

In the Days of Buell

After the withdrawal of Alexander, his lands in Muhlenberg County were placed into the charge of Colonel S. P. Love, who later became a colonel in the 11th Kentucky Infantry and who after the war was a county judge for Muhlenberg for some years. He was succeeded by Tom Bruce, a merchant and one time county clerk, who looked after Alexander's interest a short time. Along in these years, Dr. Shelby A. Jackson was in some way connected with Airdrie. Dr. Jackson was one of the most widely-known men of his day and a friend of Andrew Glenn Ferguson, both of them members of two of the oldest and best families in Muhlenberg.

David B. Roll followed Tom Bruce as agent of the land. "Squire Roll," as he was familiarly called, was a magistrate, a well-to-do farmer and stock raiser and the owner of considerable property. The overseeing of Alexander's Tract was in "Squire Roll's" hands when General Don Carlos Buell appeared on the scene.

Immediately after the close of the war, General Buell began a search for an oil field. He came to Airdrie from Marietta, Ohio, in 1866 for the sole purpose of working the oil on Alexander's lands. He took a forty year mineral and oil lease on Alexander's 17,000 acres. Alexander was, among other things, to receive one-tenth of all "the petroleum or other oil or oily substances obtained from the land." This company, of which General Buell was president, was known as Airdrie Petroleum Company.

General Buell drilled extensively on the Alexander property along Green River and also on the Buckner Furnace Tracts. On the latter place he found good deposits of iron just as Buckner and Churchill and James Gilmour had done before him. However, he made no arrangements to mine the iron ore on the latter place, for the simple reason that it was then too far from a railroad. Airdrie being on Green River and having the best transportation facilities, he decided to establish himself there.

Furthermore, after the death of Alexander, the Alexander heirs, wishing to dispose of some of his property to which they had fallen heir, entered into an agreement with General Buell whereby the General received the Airdrie furnace and about 1,000 acres around it for having released the 40 years' lease that he then held. He therefore confined his work to his own property near Airdrie.

At any rate, the coal he discovered while looking for oil was in such abundance that he changed plans and directed his attention to the coal development.

In the meantime the Bowling Green & Evansville Navigation Company or the Green River Navigation Company, or a corporation with a similar name, gained control of the Green River, which stream, up to that time, was owned by the State of Kentucky. The increased freight rate demanded of Buell was such that he could not possibly meet any of his competitors. He fought the corporation through the legislature for some 15 years. His work resulted in the Federal government purchasing Green River about the year 1887. The river was then put in good order, the old locks were improved and more new ones added.

After Buell had won his transportation rate fight he felt too far advanced in years to again begin his work of developing the mineral. Much of the machinery had gone to wreck and ruin. Some was sold. One of the boilers was bought by Fred Ames, who installed it in his first carriage works in Owensboro, which establishment later developed into one of the largest factories of its kind in the state. On one occasion an old iron peddler agreed to buy all the old pig iron and scrap iron lying around the furnace. It is said the peddler loaded his barge not only with scrap but with all the machinery on the place, except the two boilers standing there today. So, under the circumstances and in spite of the available mineral, it is not at all surprising that nothing further was undertaken.

Of all the traditions connected with Airdrie possibly none is the source of more confusion (except this five-chapter conglomeration,) than the one based on "the time the prisoners were worked at Airdrie." Some declare Alexander worked them in his mines; others say General Buell used them in connection with his work. One young man's idea was that General Buell here held the prisoners he captured in the Civil War. A number of people are under the impression the Stone House was built by and for some of the state convicts. As a matter of fact, it was erected in 1855 by Alexander for the exclusive purpose of using it for certain machinery. One can hear anything and everything in regard to the prisoners except that they were brought over from Scotland by Alexander.

The truth of the matter, however, is this. About 1884 when the Eddyville prison was being built, arrangements had been made with General Buell to quarry stone on his place to be used in the new prison building. Some fifteen prisoners were sent by the state for the purpose of getting out the rock, who while at Airdrie were quartered in the Stone House. They remained only a few months, for in the meantime other stone had been discovered by General Lyon near Eddyville and the state then transferred the prisoners to the new quarry.

The stories of prisoners being worked by the owners of Airdrie are as groundless as those circulating over the country regarding the kinship and friendship that existed between General Buell and General Bragg. Without going into details, I will say that those two soldiers were not related by blood or marriage and did not sleep in the same bed the night before the battle of Perryville.

General Buell lived in the old house built by William McLean. His wife before her marriage was a Mrs. Mason, the mother of Miss Nannie Mason. She died on August 10, 1881. After Mrs. Buell's death, Mrs. Course, the General's sister, made the place her home until 1885, when she died. General Buell died in the same house at Airdrie on November 19, 1898, and his body was sent to Belfountain Cemetery at St. Louis, after which his stepdaughter, Miss Nannie Mason, fell heir to his estate.

Miss Nannie Mason then removed to Louisville but made many trips back to the old house. After the General's death, William Shakelton occupied the house for about two years. He was succeeded by a man named Bemis who in turn was followed by Lorenzo Griggs. John Hendrie, the then architect of the old stone structures around Airdrie, occupied the house from September, 1904, to November, 1906. Dave Rhoades came next and was living in the historic old mansion when, on the night of October 26, 1907, it was destroyed by fire.

During its seventy-five years of existence, many of Muhlenberg's old pioneers loitered under its roof. Alexander entertained a number of renowned American and foreign visitors while living there. During Buell's residence at Airdrie many men prominent in military and social circles were the guests of the General. None, no matter how humble, were received with more open arms than his neighbors and friends of the Green River country.

Old Airdrie is now owned by the "Five J Coal Company" of which Shelby J. Gish, son of Sam C. Gish, a pioneer of the county, is the manager and an extensive stock holder. The other officers of this company are W. W. Jamieson, president, and W. W. Jamieson, Jr., vice president and secretary, both of whom are from Clarksburg, W. Va. The other members of the board of directors are J. G. Cochran and J. W. Crandall of Ohio. All the above mentioned gentlemen, with F. O. Funk and Oscar Welt of West Virginia, form the "Five J Coal Company", a title derived from the five Js occurring in their names.

This corporation owns about 11,000 acres in Muhlenberg County, 4,000 of which is in the immediate vicinity of Airdrie. They have 17 miles of river front in this county. This fact, together with their easy access to the L. &. N. R. R. and the I. C. R. R. and the undisputed quantity of their coal, iron and clay, give them every advantage and assurance of a grand success.

The day is not far off when old Airdrie will rise from its grave and the same visitors who beheld its ruins and sighed at the sight of the deserted and demolished village may soon return to find on the historic old spot the thriving town of New Airdrie and, like the new Courthouse, be a credit to the county.

{The End}

The Stone House at Airdrie   The Airdrie Furnace

The Stone Steps at Airdrie in about 1898

The old hotel building at Airdrie as it appeared in 1895.

General Buell's residence at Airdrie in 1900, before it burned in 1907.

Paradise Country And Old Airdrie

By OTTO A. ROTHERT
Reprinted from his
History of Muhlenberg County, 1913

(Many paragraphs in this chapter are identical to ones found in the previous chapter. Both were written by Otto A. Rothert. The previous chapter was written for the local newspaper in 1908 — this chapter for his book which was published in 1913.)

Among the influential men who began an active career in the Paradise country during the second quarter of the last century was George W. Haden who was born in Maryland, December 6, 1813. He was a son of Joseph Haden, a pioneer of Kentucky, who at the time of the birth of his son was temporarily located in Hagerstown, Maryland. His parents made the return trip west over the mountains and through Kentucky on horseback carrying their little son George with them. George W. Haden's mill was the first sawmill erected in the vicinity of Paradise. After running a horse-power "upright saw" or "sash saw" for a number of years, he put in a circular saw run by steam, the second of its kind in the county[2]. His mill business was well established when (R. S. C. A.) Alexander began building Airdrie. He sawed all the lumber used in the erection of its

---

[2] The first steam powered sawmill and grist mill in Muhlenberg County was built on Caney Creek in 1848 by Edward Weir.

houses. He also built the first flat-boats used by the various coal operators who mined at Airdrie before the arrival of the Alexanders. Mr. Haden lived on his large farm east of Drakesboro and for almost a half century was connected with various sawmills in Muhlenberg County. He was a Southern sympathizer and made many sacrifices for the *Lost Cause*. Mr. and Mrs. Haden were the parents of Joseph C. Haden, Mrs. Amanda (J. G.) Bohannon and Roy Haden. Mr. Haden died in Greenville, November 10, 1904.

The land on which the town of Airdrie was later built was for a short time the property of Judge Alney McLean. His son, William McLean, in the latter part of the 1830s, began, near the building occupied by his father, the house afterwards known as Alexander house and which later became the Buell house. William McLean was the eldest son of Judge Alney McLean and was the first, so it is said, to work the coal around [3]Airdrie. After the death of his father in 1841, he moved his mother and her children from Greenville to his new residence. While the McLean family was living here, William McLean married. A few years later he and his wife moved south but frequently returned to visit their old home. In the meantime the mine opened by him was worked by William Duncan, of Bedford, Indiana, and J. W. Newlan, who were succeeded by Thomas Carson, of Bowling Green, who was probably the last to work the McLean coal bank before the arrival of Alexander.

In those days steamboats plied on Green River between Bowling Green and Louisville. None ever passed the McLean house without a salute. It was from the McLean landing that many Greenville and other Muhlenberg people

---

[3] It has been recorded that William McLean opened Muhlenberg County's first commercial coal mine in 1820 near the later town of Airdrie. The mine has long been known as the "McLean Old Bank".

took passage. What was, in 1846, the newest and finest boat on Green River was named *"Lucy Wing"*, in honor of the daughter of Charles Fox Wing. Captain Culliver was always in charge of this boat. It is said he was a great admirer of *"Poems by Amelia"*, and that he presented many of his passengers with copies of that work. This was a book published in 1845 by Amelia Welby, a popular Ohio poetess of that time, whose writings were exploited by George D. Prentice.

The Naming of Airdrie

Airdrie derives its name from a small city of the same name in Scotland, situated between Edinburgh and Glasgow. It is the old home of the titled Alexanders. Robert Sproul Crawford Aitcheson Alexander, the founder of Airdrie in Muhlenberg, was born in Frankfort, Kentucky, in 1819. He was a son of Honorable Robert Alexander and a grandson of Sir William Alexander and his wife, who was a Miss Aitcheson of the house of Airdrie, Scotland. The Honorable Robert's eldest brother was a bachelor and was named, like their father, William; he succeeded to the title. This Sir William, the bachelor, promised his brother Robert, then living in the Bluegrass region of Kentucky, to educate his oldest son Robert and let him succeed to the title and estate if he would send him to Scotland for that purpose. This was done, and after Sir William's death, young Robert fell heir to the estate. Some years after the death of his uncle he decided to return to America in order to be near his brother and sisters (Alexander John Alexander, Mrs. J. B. Waller and Mrs. H. C. Deeds). Besides, his supply of Black Band iron ore in Scotland was about exhausted. He made a search for similar ore in America through his geologists, Charles Hendrie, Sr., and his son, Alexander Hendrie, who discovered the existence of a desirable ore, in 1851, first near the abandoned Buckner Furnace and then near Paradise. Alexander bought about seventeen thousand acres of land in Muhlenberg County, all of which with the exception of the Buckner Furnace lay along Green River

The Beginning of Airdrie

Alexander believed the Scotch were the most competent iron-workers in the world, and so, during the latter part of 1854, he brought many of his former employees and their families to his new Airdrie. A special ship, it is said, was chartered for the trip. It required six weeks for their sailing-vessel to cross the ocean. Tradition has it that their boat had a collision with a waterlogged boat, which resulted in changing their course to such an extent that they landed at New York instead of Philadelphia. From Pittsburgh, they came down the Ohio, and after some delay in Louisville, started up the Green River. Upon arriving at Airdrie, their "New Scotland", they immediately set to work finishing the houses begun in the new town by Alexander Hendrie and a number of local masons and carpenters, among whom were Alfred Johnson and his son, Lonz Johnson, and Thomas Sumner and his son Alney McLean Sumner.

Alexander spared no expense in his work. The capital at his disposal for this undertaking was practically unlimited. It is said he invested over $350,000. He enlarged the McLean house in which he retained a few rooms for his personal use. Besides the furnace, stone house, and mill, he erected a two-story frame hotel, a few two-story frame dwellings and about 20 frame cottages of three rooms each. These houses were lathed and plastered and supplied with massive chimneys and large open fireplaces. Everybody around the works, regardless of position, was comfortably housed.

After considerable drilling, digging and delaying, the furnace was finally started. Alexander, as said before, believed the Scotch were the most competent iron-workers in the world, and he therefore gave them full sway. While his men may have been thoroughly familiar with the handling of the Black Band iron ore in Scotland, they evidently did not realize the ore here required a different treatment. Three or four unsuccessful attempts were made to run the furnace. The trouble lay not in the ore, but in its management. Had they changed some of their methods, the probabilities are that the undertaking would have been a grand success.

Alexander's patience soon gave out. He cared very little about the money involved, for it was only a small part of his fortune. He set a date for the discontinuing of the work, and although the drillers discovered more iron ore on the preannounced day, Alexander nevertheless clung to his firm resolution and abandoned the work. This was in the fall of 1857. He retired to his stock farm near Lexington, where he did probably more than any other man toward the improvement of blooded stock in this state. At the time of his death on his farm December 1, 1867, he was reputed to be the richest man in Kentucky.

Sir Robert S. C. Aitcheson Alexander was a bachelor. After the death of his uncle he became known as *Lord Alexander*. He was a quiet, modest unassuming man. His employees called him "the *lord*". On one occasion a backwoodsman named Williams paid a visit to Airdrie, and upon his arrival immediately asked for "that there *Lord*". Alexander was pointed out to him. Williams sashayed around him and sized him up from head to foot and then expressed his astonishment by saying, "So you are the *Lord*, are you? By gum, you are nothin' but a human bein' after all, and a plain, ordinary, say-little sort of a feller at that. They said you was a Big Bug, but five foot six will reach you any day in the week, by Washington!" This amused Alexander, for he realized how unconsciously but truthfully the speaker had described him. He gave Williams a hearty hand shake, and a few weeks later the backwoodsman presented "Lord Elick" with "enough venison for all Scotland".

Airdrie A Happy Colony

Notwithstanding the fact that the furnace was a failure from a commercial standpoint, life in the colony was happy. Although the men spent most of their time at work connected with the mines and furnace and the women were occupied with their household affairs, amusements of many sorts were frequent. The women attended afternoon gatherings of various sorts and did much toward introducing new customs among the native families with whom they came in contact. The men were good fishermen and splendid swimmers. Archie Pollock, one of the jolliest of the Scotlanders, was the "champion fist-fighter". In fact, friendly fist fights were on the program more than any other sport. Dances were frequently given. Some of the old Scotch airs introduced by them can still be heard at the "old fiddler's contests" occasionally held in the county.

Although the town of Airdrie was short-lived, its establishment resulted in the introduction of many new and desirable families into Muhlenberg. After the withdrawal of Alexander, practically all the men and women who came from Scotland remained in the county and are today represented by many descendants.

The Men Who Ran Airdrie

Andrew Duncan and his brothers, Robert and David Duncan, left Scotland for America in the early part of 1855, and a few months later Alexander sent for them to come to Airdrie. They were practical miners, and Alexander gave them a contract to sink a shaft. One of the brothers managed the day shift and the other the night crew. William G. Duncan, now the best-known mine operator in Kentucky, is a son of Andrew Duncan, and David John Duncan, the well-known insurance man of Greenville, is the son of David Duncan.

James Gilmour (Gilmore) and his brother Matthew Gilmour were among Alexander's trusted employees. James spent most of his life in the Paradise country and died there in 1895. James G. Gilmour of Paradise, is his son. Matthew returned to Scotland and there managed a large coal mine.

Robert Kipling, the patternmaker, was an Englishman and came to Airdrie with Frank Toll. After the works were abandoned, he located on a farm near Paradise where he died March 10, 1902. Among his children now living in the county are Miss M. Bettie, Miss Rhoda A., George S., and R. Henry Kipling. Kipling, like every other man in Airdrie, was an admirer of J. Jack Robertson of the upper Pond Creek country. Kipling designed and cast a number of door-props called *"Old Jack Robertson"*. They were iron figures about ten inches long and five inches high, representing "Old Jack" sitting on the floor with his legs stretched out, a goose between them, and he in the act of carving it. A few of these iron door-weights can still be found in the county.

Hendrie the Geologist

Alexander Hendrie was Alexander's geologist. His father, Charles Hendrie, Sr., was manager of the estates belonging to the House of Airdrie. Alexander Hendrie, or "Scotch Henry", was born in Airdrie, Scotland, June 24, 1820. In 1848 he came to the United States in search of iron ore for Alexander. In 1850, he located in Paducah where by prearrangement he met his father with whom he made an exploration of the deposits of iron ore in western Kentucky. In the course of a few months they began an investigation of the Buckner Furnace tract and there found the ore that they considered was what they were looking for. Their recommendation of the iron ore on this tract resulted in Alexander buying the place in 1851.

Hendrie, wishing to be near his work, moved into the abandoned Buckner house which he had restored for that purpose. While living near The Stack he occupied some of his leisure time farming. In the meantime he explored various parts of the county and, among other places, discovered iron ore near Paradise. Alexander visited Hendrie on the Buckner place and discussed with him the questions of quality, quantity and location of the iron ores on the various tracts that had been bought. Hendrie advised Alexander not to repair The (Buckner) Stack, where transportation facilities were an obstacle, but to build a new furnace on Green River. In 1853 they selected a site below Paradise and named it Airdrie. Hendrie, assisted by Matthew Gilmour, immediately began the new town. Alexander Hendrie's brother, John Hendrie, while still in Scotland, drew the plans for the new furnace and stone house.

About 1853, Alexander Hendrie moved to Airdrie. In the meantime, he superintended the farming on the Buckner place. He continued to look after that tract until he resigned as manager of the Airdrie furnace. He made many trips between the two places on his celebrated mare, "Susie". This animal was burned to death while hitched in one of the Buckner stables; however, shortly after, George W. Haden presented him with a mare, "Dolly", that for many years was considered one of the most beautiful and intelligent animals in the county. Alexander Hendrie had a good education and, notwithstanding one report to the contrary, was a sober and industrious man. Tradition says his only fault lay in the fact that he was "too good for his own good". After his resignation as manager of Airdrie, he continued to visit Lexington where he was invariably the guest of his friend Alexander. Shortly after he left Airdrie he became connected with the Riverside mine where he remained until about 1864 when he moved to his farm in

Ohio County, where he died in May, 1874. One of his sons is Charles Hendrie, the well-known mining engineer of Central City.

John Macdougal, the father of William Macdougal, was also among those who held responsible positions at Airdrie. Gilbert Muir, the father-in-law of James Gilmour, was the "driver" or engineer and retained charge of the machinery long after the furnace was abandoned. Robert Patterson was the bookkeeper and also one of the civil engineers. It was he who surveyed a line from Airdrie, while the furnace was in operation, to the old Buckner Furnace, from which place Alexander was planning to get ore. Henry Southerland was a shoemaker in Scotland and continued in that line of work at Airdrie and Paradise.

William Torrence was the engine-builder, in which capacity he had also worked in Scotland. Shortly before the works were abandoned, he became one of the overseers. After the place was shut down, he farmed across Green River from Airdrie. At the breaking out of the war, Torrence became a member of Company I, Eleventh Kentucky Infantry, and later settled in Rockport where he died. Frank Toll held various positions at the furnace.

Much has been written about Airdrie. As far as I am aware, the sketches that have been published are all, with one exception, nothing more than absurd murder and ghost stories that evidently originated in the minds of those who wrote them. The exception I refer to is *"A Report Upon the Airdrie Furnace and Property",* republished by the Kentucky State Geological Survey from an original record made in 1874 by P. N. Moore to Professor N. S. Shaler, then in charge of the survey. It is a report of twenty-eight pages on the character of the coal and iron resources on Airdrie property. One page is devoted to description of the furnace and about three pages to its history. These I quote:

-

A Report Upon the Airdrie Furnace and Property

The furnace was built in 1855-56. It has an iron shell stack, resting upon a masonry base, twenty-six and a half feet square by twenty-one feet high. The outside diameter of the shell is twenty-three feet. The internal dimensions of the furnace are as follows: height fifty feet, diameter of bosh twenty-four feet *(bosh cylindrical for six feet),* diameter of throat eleven feet. The hearth is four feet high *(elliptical in shape),* seven feet four inches by (about) five feet. The furnace is entirely open-topped, having no facilities for saving the gases, and requiring separate firing for both boilers and hot blasts. There are two hot-blast ovens of the old-fashioned pistol-pipe pattern, with thirty-four pipes in each oven, ten curved pipes on each side, with seven straight at each end. The pipes are eight feet long, elliptical in cross-section, nine by eighteen inches, with diaphragm through the center of each.

There are four boilers, each forty inches in diameter by twenty-eight feet in length, each boiler having two flues. The engine is vertical, with direct connection between the steam and blast cylinders, and also connected with a heavy walking-beam and fly-wheel, the walking-beam working with a counterpoise at one end.

The steam cylinder is twenty inches in diameter and nine feet stroke; the blast cylinder six feet ten inches in diameter, stroke same as steam cylinder.

The engine-house is a splendid stone structure, built of fine freestone, which occurs at the furnace. Everything about the furnace is constructed in the most thorough and durable manner.

The top of the furnace is about the level of the No. 11 Coal, to be hereafter described, and the ore and coal from the No. 12 seam were brought to the furnace mouth through

40

a tunnel cut in the No. 11 Coal. The engine is in good order and well preserved.

The furnace proper stands perfectly sound (1874) and could, in a very brief time, be put in condition to go into blast; but among the buildings attached thereto, the lapse of many years since they were in use has not been without its effect, so that repairs to the buildings and hot blast apparatus will need to be made before they can be used again.

The Airdrie Furnace property consists of about 17,000 acres of land in Muhlenberg County, Kentucky. This land is not all in one body, but lies in various sized lots, ranging from 500 to 5,000 acres. The greater portion of the estate lies within a short distance of the furnace; but one tract of about 5,000 acres — the old Buckner Furnace property — is about five miles from Greenville, the county seat of Muhlenberg County, and fifteen miles from Airdrie.

Having thus considered in detail the resources of this property, and seen the remarkable advantages it possesses for obtaining fuel and cheap and varied supplies of ores, the question naturally presents itself: why then, with all these advantages, was the furnace no more successful on its former trial? This is a serious and important question, for the reproach of failures laid against an enterprise of this kind outweighs many advantages.

Into the answer a number of reasons enter, and to render them properly understood, it will be necessary to go into the history of the former campaign of the furnace in some detail, and to refer to the management of the enterprise in language which is unmistakable, although it may seriously reflect upon the business sagacity of some persons once connected with it who are no longer living. It should be premised that the information upon which the following account is based was obtained partly from the books of the furnace and partly from men who were on the ground, connected with the furnace in various capacities.

The enterprise seems to have been conceived by its proprietor in a spirit in which benevolence, national pride, and the desire for a profitable investment were strangely mingled. Being a Scotchman, and having some knowledge of iron manufacture as practiced in Scotland, he not unnaturally believed men of that nationality to be the most competent and desirable persons to conduct establishment of iron making.

He, therefore, committed from the beginning the serious mistake of employing almost exclusively newly arrived foreigners, men who, however competent at home, were without any knowledge of American prices and metallurgical practice or experience with American ores and fuel.

Having found what was firmly believed to be the equivalent of the celebrated Scotch Black Band iron ore, and an associate coal which it was thought could be used raw in the furnace, he proceeded to erect a furnace modeled after the Scotch pattern. He brought over large numbers of Scotch miners and furnace men and employed them almost exclusively; giving them to understand, it is reported, that it was to improve their condition rather than in hopes of great returns, that he had made the investment. He employed as superintendent and manager an uneducated, dissipated Scotchman, a man wholly unfit to fill so important and responsible a position, and to him gave almost entire charge of the whole enterprise, often not visiting the property for months at a time.

Under such conditions, it is no wonder that there was mismanagement, and that ill-advised expenditures were made.

For three years, while the slow process of development was going on, the furnace and machinery erected, entries driven, and the great shaft, five and a half by eighteen feet, sunk to a depth of four hundred and thirty feet in search of a mythical ore (known to exist fifteen miles distant and no where between) the proprietor continued uncomplainingly to increase his investment.

At last the furnace was started. It ran a few days unsuccessfully, producing iron of a poor quality and in small amount, when an accident to the boiler compelled it to be blown out.

Repairs were made in due time and the furnace again started. The working was no better than before, and the iron not improved in quality or quantity. In twenty-two days from the time of starting the saddle-plate of the walking-beam broke, disabling the engine and compelling the furnace to be shoveled out. Again it started, and again, after a short run, no more successful than the last, an accident happened to the engine, the cast-iron shaft of the fly-wheel broke, and once more the furnace was shoveled out.

In all three of these unfortunate campaigns, the furnace was not in blast altogether more than six weeks or two months.

After the last blast, the manager concluded that the coal did not work well raw, and so made a large amount of coke from it to be tried in the next blast, but the next blast never came; the proprietor's patience was exhausted; he stopped the operations entirely, discharged his men, and shut up the mines and the furnace.

Since that time (November 1857) the furnace has never been in operation. The No. 11 Coal has been worked largely for shipment to the Southern market, but beyond that the property has been lying idle and unproductive.

The closing of the furnace at that time was a mistake no less serious than some committed in starting it. The manager was beginning to learn, by the only method by which a so-called practical, uneducated man can learn —

43

his own dear-bought experience — that American ores and fuel are not exactly like the Scotch, and that different practice is required for their treatment. Had he been allowed to go on, using coke for fuel, it is not unlikely that his next campaign would have proved much more successful.

It can be truly said that the furnace has never been subjected to a fair trial. A total campaign of six weeks or two months, divided into three short blasts, affords no fair basis for judgment as to the merits of furnace, fuel or ore.

General Buell Enters Picture

After the withdrawal of Alexander, his lands in Muhlenberg County were placed in charge of Colonel S. P. Love. He was succeeded by Thomas Bruce, a merchant and one-time county clerk, who looked after Alexander's interest a short time. Along in these years, Doctor Shelby A. Jackson was in someway connected with Airdrie. Doctor Jackson was one of the most widely known men of his day. David B. Roll followed Thomas Bruce as agent of the land. "Squire" Roll, as he was familiarly called, was a magistrate for ten years in succession, a well-to-do farmer and stock raiser, and the owner of considerable property. The overseeing of the Alexander tracts was in Squire Roll's hand when General Don Carlos Buell appeared on the scene.

Immediately after the close of the war, General Buell began a search for an oil field. He came to Airdrie from Marietta, Ohio in 1868, for the sole purpose of working the oil on the Alexander lands. He took a forty-year mineral and oil lease on Alexander's seventeen thousand acres. Alexander was to receive, among other things, one tenth of all "the petroleum or other oil or oily substance obtained from the land". This company, of which General Buell was president, was known as the Airdrie Petroleum Co.

Buell drilled extensively on the Alexander property along Green River and also on the Buckner Furnace tract. Airdrie being on Green River and having the best transportation facilities, he decided to establish himself there. Furthermore, after the death of Alexander, the Alexander heirs, wishing to dispose of some of the property which they had inherited, entered into an agreement with Buell whereby the latter received a deed on the Airdrie furnace and about a thousand acres around it for having released the forty-year lease that he then held. However, the coal Buell discovered while looking for oil was in such abundance that he changed his plans and directed most of his attention to the coal development.

In the meantime (1868) The Green and Barren Rivers Navigation Company leased Green River, which stream up to that time had been directly controlled by the State of Kentucky. The increased freight rate demanded by the new corporation was so much that Buell could not meet the prices of his competitors, to whom a lower freight rate was given. He fought this corporation through the Legislature for some fifteen years. His long, hard, and sometime time-sacrificing work resulted in the Federal government purchasing the unexpired lease of the Navigation Company in 1888. The river was then put in good order and the old locks were improved and new ones added. For this work alone, he deserves a monument.

After Buell had won his transportation rate fight, he felt too far advanced in years to again begin his work of developing the mines. In the meantime much of the machinery had gone to wreck and ruin, and some of it had been sold. One one occasion, it is said, an old iron peddler agreed to buy all the old pig iron and scrap iron lying around the furnace. The peddler loaded his barge, however, not only with scrap but with all the machinery on the place except for two boilers standing there today. Under the circumstances, and in spite of the available minerals, it is not at all surprising that nothing further was undertaken by General Buell.

Stories of Prisoners Exaggerated

Of all the extravagant stories told about Airdrie, few are more absurd than those relative to the Stone House, sometimes — but erroneously — referred to as the Old Prison. Some declare Alexander worked prisoners in the mines; others say Buell used them in connection with his work. One young man's idea was that Buell here held the prisoners he had captured in the Civil War. A number of people are under the impression that the Stone House was built by and for some of the state convicts. In fact, one can hear anything and everything in regard to the "prisoners" except that they were free workmen brought over from Scotland by Alexander.

The truth of the matter, however, is this: About 1884, when Eddyville prison was being enlarged, arrangements were made with General Buell to quarry stone on his place, to be used in the new penitentiary. About fifteen prisoners were sent by the state for the purpose of getting out the rock, who while at Airdrie were quartered in the Stone House. They remained only a few weeks, for in the meantime other stone had been discovered by General Lyon near Eddyville, and the state then transferred the prisoners to the new quarry.

Many ghost stories are connected with the old hotel building at Airdrie. It was the largest frame house erected by Alexander. It remained unoccupied after Alexander abandoned the furnace, and its weather-beaten walls, broken windows, and generally dilapidated condition gave rise to a report that the place was haunted. Although all traces of the hotel have disappeared, the ghost stories have continued to increase in number and variety. Many of them begin with a murder scene and end with the maneuvers of

46

a headless ghost. No one was ever killed in or near the building, all reports to the contrary notwithstanding.

The stories of the haunted hotel and of "prisoners" being worked by the owners of Airdrie are as groundless as those circulated over the county regarding the kinship or friendship between General Buell and General Bragg. Those two soldiers were not related by blood or marriage and did not "sleep in the same bed the night before the battle of Perryville". General Buell on November 19, 1851, married the widow of General Richard Barnes Mason, who was a grandson of General George Mason of Revolutionary fame. General Bragg's wife was Miss Ellis of Louisiana. General Buell's wife before her second marriage was Mrs. Margaret (Turner) Mason, the mother of Miss Nannie Mason. Mrs. Buell died in Airdrie on August 10, 1881. After her death, Mrs. Crouse, the general's sister, made the place her home until 1885, when she died. General Buell died at Airdrie on November 19, 1898, and his body was sent to Belfontaine Cemetery, St. Louis. His estate was willed to Miss Nannie Mason who, a few years after his death, made Louisville her home. In 1908 she sold the Airdrie land to the Five J Coal Company, of which Shelby J. Gish of Central City was general manager.

After the General's death, William Shackelton occupied the house for about two years. He was succeeded by Lorenzo D. Griggs. John Hendrie, then the aged architect of the old stone structures at Airdrie, occupied the house from September, 1904, to November, 1906. David Rhoads came next and was living in the historic old mansion when, on the night of October 26, 1907, it was destroyed by fire.

During its seventy-five years of existence, many of Muhlenberg's pioneers loitered under its roof. Alexander entertained American and foreign visitors while living there. Charles Eaves was General Buell's most intimate friend in the county and likewise his frequent visitor. During Buell's residence in Airdrie, many men prominent in military and social circles were his guests. None, however, no matter how distinguished, was received with more open arms than his neighbors and friends of the Green River country.

* * *

(Reprinted in part from Otto Rothert's History of Muhlenberg County, published in 1913.)

The Mill Stacks
at Airdrie
as Otto Rothert
saw them about
1900.

Abandoned houses at Airdrie as they appeared in 1895.

Airdrie's Post Office
(1856-1859)

The town of Airdrie, site of the historic Airdrie stack, once had its own post office. After the building of the Airdrie iron works and stack near Paradise in 1855, the post office department established a postal center at Airdrie on May 21, 1856. Like the town of Airdrie which failed to thrive after the iron works were closed, the Airdrie post office also fell on hard times and was discontinued on May 26, 1859, with postal service reverting to the Paradise office.

The only postmaster to serve Airdrie was Samuel Heath, a Scottish immigrant.

Residents in the Airdrie area were served by the Paradise post office prior to the establishment of the office at Airdrie. The Paradise post office was established on March 1, 1852, with Robert Duncan the postmaster. After William Wand succeeded Mr. Duncan in 1853, the office was discontinued on March 21, 1856, because of the rapid build-up at Airdrie and the establishment of the Airdrie post office. All mail in that area then was diverted through the new Airdrie post office.

However, the iron ore business soon failed at Airdrie, and after struggling several years, the post office business also faltered. The town of Airdrie succumbed to these hard times, and both the post office and the town disappeared from the map.

On May 26, 1859, the post office was returned to Paradise where it remained, with one possible interruption in 1865, until it was finally closed on November 17, 1967.

The notation was made in federal postal records that the office closed in 1865 — but a later notation indicated that the office had continued with no interruption.

Other postmasters who served the Paradise office included: Jared Brown, Elvis G. Hill, Samuel L. James, Robert Glenn, Joseph Fox, Andrew Duncan, Robert C. Duncan, Henry C. Fox, John Ham, Bettie Wallace, William S. Fox, Mary Humphrey, Martha D. Fox, and the final postmaster, John Herman Buchanan, who served from 1940 to 1967.

The post office in Paradise was closed in 1967 after the coming of the Paradise TVA steam plant to the banks of Green River. This caused the complete demolishment and removal of the pioneer town of Paradise, earlier known in Muhlenberg County history as Stums (or Stom's) Landing. *(Bobby Anderson*

General Buell's residence, private park, and boat landing.

Old Kentucky Iron Furnaces

Reprinted from an early edition of the
Filson Club Quarterly

Aylette H. Buckner, father of General Simon Bolivar Buckner, after operating a small furnace near his home, Glen Lily, on the banks of Green River in Hart County, moved to Muhlenberg County where there was an extensive bed of iron ore and a plentiful supply of timber. With Cadwalader Churchill, he formed a large company and built the furnace stack (1837) near the junction of Pond Creek and Salt Lick Creek, five miles south of Greenville. Before the end of the following year, operations had begun for the manufacture of iron. This furnace was variously known as the "Henry Clay Iron Works", Buckner's Stack, and Buckner & Churchill's Furnace. A gristmill was built near the stack, numerous cabins were erected for white and slave laborers, and a small, almost self-sufficient village grew up around the furnace.

Despite the great abundance of ore and timber, the company began to have financial troubles by the time it fairly got into business. The venture was on too large a scale for a remote region in the pioneer days. The great expense of getting ores to the stack, of burning charcoal, of finding markets, and strong competition from other sections in Kentucky more favorably situated, caused the Buckner & Churchill Company to fail financially; the furnace was abandoned in the year 1842.

A more ambitious undertaking was the Airdrie Furnace, erected in the northeastern section of Muhlenberg County in 1855, on the banks of Green River, near the village of Paradise. Sir Robert S. C. A. Alexander, a Kentucky-born descendant of a wealthy, titled Scotch family, purchased 17,000 acres of heavily wooded land in this area where a large bed of iron ore had been discovered. Young

Alexander brought over from his father's country a number of Scotch miners and furnace men to help him develop the Muhlenberg County area. Arriving late in the summer of 1854, they built houses and cottages for the workmen and erected a large, cylindrical iron-shell stack, 48 feet high resting on a 26-foot square stone base, 20 feet high, together with a huge three-story sandstone building to house the machinery for furnace blast and rolling mills. The whole establishment was modeled after the Scotch pattern.

Looking upward toward the third story and the stone work in the Airdrie powerhouse. These stones have been standing in place since they were laid by Alfred Johnson and his son Lonz, in 1855.

Four or five unsuccessful attempts were made to run the furnace. The Scotch workmen were unfamiliar with Kentucky metallurgical practices; the ore required a different treatment from that found in Scotland. After spending more than three hundred thousand dollars without being able to produce a single pound of saleable iron, *"Lord Alexander"* abandoned the project in disgust and retired to a large Bluegrass farm he had purchased in Woodford County. The town of Airdrie was short-lived; and in a few years all the houses, stores, and the settlement's two-story hotel were in ruins.

* * *

Editor's note: For more information on the Buckner Stack in Muhlenberg County, read Otto Rothert's "History of Muhlenberg County", published in 1913.

AIRDRIE

(From The Green River Country,
published in 1898 by J. S. Reilly.)
Edited by W. P. Greene

This is one of the most interesting spots on Green River. Not because of any particular charm arising from natural location or artificial embellishment, but because it is and has been for many years, the home of America's illustrious citizens. At the close of the civil war General D. C. Buell retired from public life and sought seclusion here upon the rugged banks of Green River. The motive for this seclusion has never passed the breath of General Buell. The fact remains that here in the calm and quiet of his woods and farms this almost lone survivor of the great leaders of the Union army is content to spend the evening of

McLean Spring at Airdrie, 1900

life. The house and grounds of Airdrie are located upon the crest of a moderately high bluff on the left hand bank of the river, about one mile below Paradise.

The latter is its post town. The dwelling house at Airdrie is a two-story frame with wide central hall and wing extending back, containing dining room, kitchen and storerooms. A veranda spans the front of the house from which is obtained a view of the river for a considerable distance up and down. A narrow lawn, set with flower beds and flanked by forest trees, descends somewhat steeply from the front porch of the house to the river bank. The view of Airdrie from the river is impaired by the presence of these trees and other low growth near the water's edge. Airdrie is not

General Don Carlos Buell

a grand place made resplendent by the still of the architect, the sculptor's chisel or the painter's brush. No special effort has been bestowed upon its ornamentation. It is simply the plain and unpretentious home of a cultured gentleman. Graveled walks extending to different parts of the forest covered the ground, and whitewashed arbors reached by rustic bridges over intervening ravines make up the sum of human infringement on nature's domain. The untrimmed woods, canopying moss-grown bands and tenanted by nature's choirs, seem to accord best with the mood of the master of Airdrie. The melodies of circling groves, the softly flowing river, the vine-draped cliffs, the subdued sounds of forest life and the peaceful calm that rests upon all are in harmony with the spirit that turned him aside from the hurrying multitude of his fellow men. General Buell is nearing, if not already past, his three score and ten years, but he does not look his age. The life forces inherited from a hardy ancestry and conserved by the abstemious life have operated to prolong his physical and mental vigor beyond that of ordinary men. He is a strict disciplinarian, as might be expected from his education and training, subjecting himself and household to a regular round of duties and labors. Ordinarily, his time is divided between his farms, his poultry, of which he is an enthusiastic breeder, and his library. He is not a recluse by any means. His splendid engineering talent and military knowledge have made his service desirable to the government in connection with the public work now proceeding at Shiloh battlefield. Beyond the time spent in the execution of this commission, he seldom goes abroad. He occasionally visits points in his neighborhood, where he is an interesting figure, on account of his soldiery bearings and martial appearance on horseback. He is much addicted to horseback exercise, a habit acquired during his campaigning days and persevered in for its healthfulness and exhilarating effect. Dressed in high top boots, slouch hat and coat buttoned to the chin and sitting on his horse like a centaur and cantering rapidly along a forest road, one could imagine him at the head of his troops hurrying to the relief of the beaten and demoralized Union forces on the night succeeding the first day's battle of Shiloh. The General takes a deep interest in public affairs, especially in the matters affecting the interest of his immediate section. He is greatly interested in the development of the agricultural and mineral resources of the Green River country. He has a most thorough and scientific knowledge of the mineral wealth of this portion of the state of

Kentucky, having devoted years to investigations relative to this branch of her resources.

In person, General Buell is about five feet, ten inches in stature, sparely, though sturdily built, and weighs about one hundred and fifty pounds His carriage is erect and his motions active, yet deliberate. His manner is reserved, though not unsocial. His general bearing in social converse is that of thoughtfulness tending to introspection. He is a ready, though not fluent conversationalist, and impresses one as being incapable of indulging in light talk or humor. The portrait accompanying this sketch is from a photograph taken in 1864 and is the only profile likeness of General Buell in existence. It recalls a dark hour in the history of our country, but it also reminds us of a bit of love and veneration we owe to the noble spirits who stood as the nation's bulwark of safety while the fearful shadows passed. Time has seared the wounds of fratricidal strife and drawn its flower-wrought robe over fields sodden with the blood of brothers, but it has not effaced from the minds of the survivors of the struggle a shuddering sense of its horrors and a tender reverence for its heroes.

Airdrie Remembered
(Author Unknown)

Note: The author of the following historical account of Airdrie is unknown. Three pages of typewritten text were passed on by a party unknown to the editor of this booklet many years ago. Thus far it has not been determined who authored the text, whether it was first written in long hand and then transcribed on a typewriter, or if it came down to paper through dictation. Nevertheless, despite a few errors in fact, it is a very interesting first-hand account of the building and demise of "Old Airdrie". It is believed that this was written about 1919-1920.

* * *

About the year 1853, R. A. Alexander, a native of Scotland, bought a tract of land near Paradise, Muhlenberg County, Kentucky, known as the McLain (McLean) Survey, being the same land on which McLain (William McLean) opened a coal mine some years previous to selling to Alexander. McLain mined coal, loaded it on flat boats and floated it to New Orleans. The coal was known as No. 11. Alexander brought some fifty to sixty families over from Scotland and established homes for them about one-half mile below or north of Paradise. They immediately went to work building dwellings, stores, barns, and other necessary buildings for permanent homes. All the men were expert mechanics, engineers, stone masons, carpenters, businessmen and architects.

After their homes were made comfortable, they turned to the work of preparing for elaborate iron works, patterned after the works owned by Alexander in Scotland. They built a dressed stone house for an engine room. It was two stories high, had a solid stone wall across the center, and was covered with slate. Every stone in the building was dressed by hand and hoisted to place by windlasses (sic) turned by manpower. They had an engine built in Scotland, as were the boilers, and shipped to New Orleans, then up the Mississippi, Ohio and Green rivers in barges, and discharged within a few hundred feet of the engine room. The engine was about seven feet long and twelve or fourteen inches in diameter. It was set on end in the northeast corner of the room, the upper ending being level with the floor. The boilers were two-flued, and there were eighteen of them, set in two batteries of nine each.They were placed near the south end of the engine room at the foot of a flight of stone steps running to the level of the tunnel through the hill. There was a casting, weighing tons, balanced on the center wall of the engine room, one end of which was attached to a piston of the engine and the other to a fly-wheel that was twenty-five feet in diameter. Pump pistons for water and air were attached to this casting (called a walking beam). Between the engine

After their homes were made comfortable, they turned to the work of preparing for elaborate iron works, patterned after the works owned by Alexander in Scotland. They built a dressed stone house for an engine room. It was two stories high, had a solid stone wall across the center, and was covered with slate. Every stone in the building was dressed by hand and hoisted to place by windlasses (sic) turned by manpower. They had an engine built in Scotland, as were the boilers, and shipped to New Orleans, then up the Mississippi, Ohio and Green rivers in barges, and discharged within a few hundred feet of the engine room. The engine was about seven feet long and twelve or fourteen inches in diameter. It was set on end in the northeast corner of the room, the upper ending being level with the floor. The boilers were two-flued, and there were eighteen of them, set in two batteries of nine each.They were placed near the south end of the engine room at the foot of a flight of stone steps running to the level of the tunnel through the hill. There was a casting, weighing tons, balanced on the center wall of the engine room, one end of which was attached to a piston of the engine and the other to a fly-wheel that was twenty-five feet in diameter. Pump pistons for water and air were attached to this casting (called a walking beam). Between the engine room and the bluff there was a large water reservoir that would hold thousands of gallons of water; also a large tank for storage of oil, which was forced into it by the pumps. The tank was about forty feet long and in the shape of a huge boiler. On this tank was a safety valve that would open at a certain pressure, and the escaping air from this valve could be heard for miles. It annoyed the whole country for ten miles around and was very disagreeable, disturbing the rest of the people, especially the sick. From this tank, the air passed through a furnace where it was heated to an extremely high temperature. A small hole was made in one of the pipes to test the hot air before it was forced into the smelting furnace nearby. The hole was not larger than a cambric needle. Open it and pass a bar of lead across it and the hot air would cut it in two so quickly that you could not see it.

The smelting stack was built up level with the mine opening and the ore and coal were wheeled by hand from the yard and dumped into it. The coal was charred before it was used. The iron ore was mined something like a half mile west of the furnace and was trammed through the hill by mule power. After the ore was melted, the stack was tapped, the molten mass was run out through a ditch or canal made of sand, into the moulding yard, where it was allowed to cool in the moulds. The yard was located between the stack and the river in front of the stack. When the iron cooled they broke off the pig from the main lead and stacked it up ready for shipping. The stone that was used for building the engine room and the stack was quarried from the ground where they now stand. A large mill was built south of the engine room; it was about 100 feet long and 50 feet wide. A sawmill, brick mill and other machinery were placed in it. All the bricks made there were located between the engine room and the mill. They sank a shaft about a half mile west of the hill to a depth of 450 feet. I have heard it said that no one except the "bosses" knew for what it was sunk.

I lived about one mile due east from the works and was often there during its building and operation. When the furnace was in full blast, one could sit in our own yard on the darkest night and read a newspaper. Many a night I have studied my school lessons at our home by the light of the furnace. At that time the Green River country was almost a wilderness and had limited markets for such farm products as were raised. Tobacco and pork had to be marketed in New Orleans. Home consumption of garden stuff was the only market for vegetables. Airdrie was the first local market in the valley. I have delivered vegetables in Airdrie many times and it was always a cash business. We were paid in gold, principally. The gold was in denominations of $20, $10, $5, $2.50 and $1; silver in 3 cents, 5 cents, 10 cents, 25 cents and 50 cents and for dollars, there was the five-franc piece, a French coin worth 95 cents in

I lived about one mile due east from the works and was often there during its building and operation. When the furnace was in full blast, one could sit in our own yard on the darkest night and read a newspaper. Many a night I have studied my school lessons at our home by the light of the furnace. At that time the Green River country was almost a wilderness and had limited markets for such farm products as were raised. Tobacco and pork had to be marketed in New Orleans. Home consumption of garden stuff was the only market for vegetables. Airdrie was the first local market in the valley. I have delivered vegetables in Airdrie many times and it was always a cash business. We were paid in gold, principally. The gold was in denominations of $20, $10, $5, $2.50 and $1; silver in 3 cents, 5 cents, 10 cents, 25 cents and 50 cents and for dollars, there was the five-franc piece, a French coin worth 95 cents in gold.

The Scots were a lively lot. They soon became familiar with the natives and were always getting up amusements for the youngsters, especially dancing parties. I was about 14 years old and had never seen a dancing party. My people believed dancing was a cardinal sin, but like most youngsters, I was ready for any new thing that came down the pike. So some of my pals and I would sneak out and go to the balls, then slip back to bed in time to be called to breakfast in the morning. I learned to go through the old-fashioned cotillion, the Virginia Reel, and a few jig steps on old Airdrie Hill, and I have never been able to get it out of my system since, notwithstanding I am nearly eighty years young.

I have spent days and days wandering around and through Airdrie, and you must know that I did not wander alone. There were always numerous youngsters ready for any kind of frolic, and let me say that there were many attractive girls in Airdrie.

About the years 1857-58 the works shut down, or they found the metal was so hard that it could not be profitably worked. They then sent to St. Louis and barged in what they called black-band ore to mix with the Airdrie iron ore. They then started the works again and made one or two runs, but with little success. The war between the states came on, the works shut down and the people scattered out throughout the two counties of Muhlenberg and Ohio. Today, we have descendants of these hard-headed Scotchmen all around us, and I am glad to say that they are rated as A-1 citizens, good neighbors, honest as the day is long, first class patriots, ready to defend our flag again all commons. We need more of this class of Scots in our country.

After the war closed, General Don Carlos Buell became the owner of the land immediately in and around Airdrie. He and Dr. S. A. Jackson operated the coal mines for a time using barges to deliver, with tow boats to propel the barges instead of floating them as did the McLains. In the year 1866 the legislature ceded the navigation rights to a company for 20 years. They soon began to tax all river craft carrying products on Green River. The tariff was so high on coal that there was no profit in producing it on Green River, and the Airdrie works shut down again and have not been revived to this day.

Airdrie is now a resort for picnicking and fishing. All the machinery, houses and materials have been scrapped and sold, nothing remaining except the engine room and the stack. The slate off the roof has long since been carried away by piecemeal. Large trees have grown up in the moulding yards, in the reservoir and the brick kilns. The roads and yards are fast becoming thickets of briers and small timber, blackberries growing where it was (once) hotter than the underworld is said to be. Several years ago, the State (of Kentucky) determined to build a branch prison at Eddyville, Ky. They contracted for the stone at Airdrie, sent a lot of prisoners from Frankfort to load the stone on barges and bring it to Rockport and transfer it to cars to ship to Eddyville, but before they had shipped any stone they found that they could work the stone at less cost nearer the prison. While the convicts were at Airdrie, they were housed in the old engine room. Some years ago some writer to the Cincinnati and Louisville papers, through ignorance or willful misrepresentation, wrote Airdrie up as a penal institution. This was all out of line; it was never intended or used for a prison except as stated above.

Referring again to the people of Airdrie, I do not want to leave the impression the good Scots were immoral. They were, as a class, strictly moral, and held to the Presbyterian faith with all the tenacity of their old forebears. The Pattersons, Duncans, Heaths, Tolls, McDougals, Sneddons, Wilsons, Keiths, Williamsons, Hamiltons, Kelleys, Terrences and many other families are among the best citizens Ohio and Muhlenberg counties have. They are capable, energetic, honorable and true men and women, leaders in church and school, a little clannish in that they almost unanimously hold the Presbyterian faith, and generally practice what they preach. They make good soldiers, good mechanics, good farmers, good preachers, and above all, good neighbors.

I am one among a few men who were intimate with Old Airdrie from its first stroke on the hills of Muhlenberg County to the present date. It virtually was, and is, my native home. Many memories of my boyhood and later manhood are centered in and around Old Airdrie.

(Unsigned)

AIRDRIE

(Written about 1930. Publication unknown.)

By C. Hall Allen

The world has forgotten moss-grown and vine-tangled Old Airdrie.

Once the home of the titled Alexanders of Scotland, and later the home of Gen. Don Carlos Buell of War Between the States fame, it is to the people of Muhlenberg County just "Old Airdrie," and they pronounce it "A-drie."

Quite a number of years have passed since Airdrie was a prosperous and well-known village — the home of noted characters in the history of Kentucky and America. Decades have passed, too, since the midnight sky was red with the light of its smelting furnaces and since boats landed there and carried to the markets of the world coal mined by a company whose president was General Buell.

Airdrie was located near the little coal camp of Paradise, Muhlenberg County, and seventeen miles from Greenville, the county seat of the county. The village was built on an immense bluff overlooking Green River and at the foot of this bluff in 1855. Sir Robert Sproul Crawford Aitchenson Alexander of the House of Airdrie in Scotland opened a mine in search of the famous Black Band ore that was rapidly diminishing in his own country. Such was the beginning of Airdrie.

Sir Robert, although born in Kentucky, was educated in Scotland and received the title and estate of a very wealthy uncle who was one of the most prominent men of Scotland at that time. He was sent back to America in the early fifties to search for the Scotch Black Band ore, and he found that type of ore at Airdrie.

Believing that all the good ore workers lived in Scotland, Sir Robert chartered a boat and with lavish promises imported to Muhlenberg County the pick and choice of Scotland's workmen. Before operations were begun, more than $350,000, a fortune in those days, had been spent, the majority of it for transportation for the miners and ore workers.

The bringing of the Scotchmen to America is regarded as one of the great reasons for Airdrie's downfall. For although the men "Lord Ellick" brought to Airdrie were experienced in handling the iron ore of their own country,

The Stone House at Airdrie from an early newspaper clipping

the Muhlenberg County ore demanded an entirely different treatment from that of their native Scotland. For instance, they were in the habit of heating the smelting furnaces with green coal. After a few failures the workmen were convinced that coke would be needed, but before the fuel could be prepared, Sir Robert threw up the sponge and closed the operation.

So it happened that in November, 1857, the village of Airdrie was deserted, and it seemed for a time that it would remain that way. But not so. Gen. Don Carlos Buell came to Kentucky after the War Between the States and began prospecting for oil and obtained a lease on the Alexander acres at Airdrie.

When Sir Robert died, his heirs disposed of the Airdrie property and a thousand acres of land surrounding to General Buell for the unexpired lease. So Buell went to Airdrie to live and there remained until his death.

Finding no oil on his property, General Buell was forced to be content with the coal which underlay his entire holdings. This occupation claimed his attention for sometime, but in 1868 the Green River Navigation Company leased the river and placed a very high freight rate on anything shipped over its waters. Now this was the only outlet for

Buell's coal, and the high freight rates made it impossible for him to compete with other companies whose transportation facilities were better, so the old General began his hardest fight to attract the Federal Government toward the project. Success crowned his efforts; the Government was led to see the conditions existing and purchased the lease from the private company. It has been said that if Buell had done nothing else in his whole life this one act would have been enough to make him a famous man.

But when the transportation question had finally been settled, General Buell was so well advanced in years that he decided that it would not be wise to continue the development of his property, and so the mines were again closed. The period of idleness had wrought wreck and ruin to his machinery and to the mines themselves, and quite a sum of money would have been needed to resume operations. So no one went to Airdrie to start work where Buell left off.

General Buell died at his home overlooking the Airdrie operations November 19, 1898, after having been cared for by Mrs. Course, his sister, and Miss (Nannie) Mason, his step-daughter, after the death of his wife. The General's body was buried in Bellefontaine Cemetery, St. Louis.

The Buell estate was willed to Miss Mason, the step-daughter, who had nursed him through his declining years, and in 1908, she sold the property to the Five J Coal Company of Central City and made her home in Louisville until her death in 1912.

After Buell's death, the mansion was occupied in turn by William Shackleford, Alonza Briggs, John Hendrie, a native of Scotland and architect of all the stone houses of Airdrie, and Davis (David?) Rhodes who occupied the house on the night of October 26, 1907, when the historic old structure burned to the ground.

A visit to the Airdrie of today reveals evidence of the industry that should have thrived there. Airdrie Hill is divided into two landings. On the first is the old ore and coal mines.On the bottom landing still stands the furnace stack, an old stone house and lofty chimneys and the mill. Here, too, are found the foundations of other structures with half-grown trees growing within the enclosure that certainly must have been a house. A hundred yards from the site of the operation, Green River flows peacefully.

From the first landing of the bluff to the bottom there is a stone stairway of fifty-four steps. This stairway is not cut in the rock as might be expected but is built against the face of the perpendicular bluff, as perfect a piece of masonry as the stone house itself.

In the old stone house, machinery was kept for running the smeltery

Tradition has it that prisoners were kept there and worked in the stone quarries up the river and in the ore mine and the furnaces. Whatever this house was used for, one of the upper windows still had a rotting framework which holds iron bars across the opening.

There are local traditions and "ghost tales" of the man who hurled himself from the top of the bluff to his death at the side of the old house, and up to a few years ago natives considered the place haunted.

Then, there is the site of Buell's park, overgrown with weeds, briars and persimmon sprouts. And further along are the ruins of the old Buell mansion, marking one of Kentucky's spots of historic interest.

During its seventy-five years of existence on the brow of Airdrie Hill, many noted Kentuckians have loitered under its roof, many distinguished national characters have visited there and many noblemen from across the seas were guests of the Alexanders during their abode there.

Kentuckians visit traditional spots of national importance and dabble in the history of foreign lands. Yet they forget the home of the Alexanders and General Buell. They forget the worn steps of the stone stairway, the rock house, the mill down by the river. But their story is interesting on two continents.

The moldering stone piles of Old Airdrie will soon be gone. But still the haunting memories of the titled members of the House of Airdrie in Scotland, and of the famous old

General who rallied to the aid of Grant at Shiloh, hover over the place. The midday sun can scarce penetrate the dense foliage of the forest around it as nature drapes an obscuring veil over the spot.

Maybe there is still iron ore there that could be mined profitably.There certainly is a very rich deposit of coal which would be worth thousands of dollars on a profitable market. But the value of Old Airdrie does not lie in its natural resources.The stone house, the furnace stack, the ruins of its mill, its houses and even the stone stairway, have a historic interest that will last after the wealth of the ore and coal have been dug away from the bowels of the hill.

POWER HOUSE, above, at Airdrie, as seen from the top of the bluff. At right are the steps leading up toward the top of the bluff. Below, the entrance to the McLean Old Bank, the mine at Airdrie.

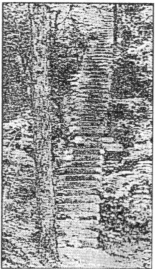

Paradise of Today Is Gaunt

Reminder of 75 Years Ago
By W. E. Daniel, Staff Writer
Owensboro, (Ky.) *Messenger-Inquirer*
(Circa 1930)

Paradise, Ky., Nov. 11 — Reports from geologists sent to America by the Alexanders of Scotland a decade before the War Between the States were responsible for the migration of Robert Alexander in 1855, from his Bluegrass stock farm in Woodford County, to the sparsely settled region bordering Green River in Muhlenberg County. Mineral outcroppings and indications of iron ore in commercial quantities were believed by the Scotland Alexanders in sufficient quantity to replace the rapidly diminishing supply of Black Band ore in that country. Emboldened by the flattering prospects, Robert Alexander quit the ancestral estates near Spring Station, between Frankfort and Versailles, and with a company of trained iron workers dispatched from Europe by his uncle, Lord Alexander, whose title he was to inherit, descended the Ohio and barged up Green River with their goods and chattels to the point where the ruins of Airdrie mark the spot selected for building an industrial city patterned after Airdrie in Scotland.

Robert Alexander was educated in Scotland by his uncle, Lord Alexander. He enjoyed the luxury of his horse

The furnace at Airdrie from an old newspaper

breeding farm in central Kentucky, to which he returned from college. But the promise of the rich uncle to finance a plan to develop the iron ore along Green River was too fascinating a prospect to deter the young nephew. He spent recklessly. A townsite was laid out. Hotels were built. Coal mines were opened and veterans from Scotland hoisted a small lot of iron ore. A blast furnace was built. A stone power house was equipped to operate the machinery. A long flight of stone steps led from the lower level near the river whereupon stood the furnace and power house to the higher lands along which stretched the well-laid-out streets of the city of Airdrie.

But developing a new industrial section did not appeal to the young Bluegrass aristocrat. The rude outlines of a raw land were less inviting than the undulant fields of his stock farm, and after spending $350,000 of his uncle's money in two years, he tired of the monotony and went home to his horses, to his elegant mansion with the spring nearby. Behind him, Robert Alexander left the immigrants who had come from Scotland to people the wooded lands, to build an industrial domain in keeping with the dignity of Lord Alexander's across the sea. Most of them remained:

the Duncans, the McDougals, the Vanland-inghams, the Hadens, the Smiths and others. Life was simple and they turned from mining, which never yielded a competence, to farming the new land. Their homes were well furnished. They had stores of all kinds needed in the village: dry goods, groceries, hardware, with sawmills, planing mills and various industries on a small scale. Life moved quietly at Airdrie, despite the loss of the promoter who never returned from his Woodford County home.

Buell Leases Airdrie

Meanwhile, the war came and went, and General Don Carlos Buell, native of Ohio, who had soldiered through Kentucky, heard of Airdrie and saw possibilities in the dormant dream of Alexander. In 1866 the General leased the 17,000 acres of Alexander lying along the river, and the Buckner furnace farm a few miles away. He organized the Airdrie Petroleum Company, and with a whim as wild as that of Alexander's, saw a fortune in oil and iron. The blast furnace was not used, nor the powerhouse His lease would extend 40 years. He established his home in the old McLean house built in the 1830s, a rambling, palatial place overlooking the river. It was situated on a 60-acre park, wherein the General cultivated flowers and shrubbery, transforming the rolling lands into a park-like expanse, extending to the water's edge.

Impractical in the extreme, the General turned from oil to coal, and one lone tunnel, penetrating the hillside near the blast furnace and power house of Alexander's day, remains. That was after the Alexander heirs, following his death in 1867, deeded General Buell 1,000 acres including the McLean house and townsite of Airdrie, in exchange for the surrender of the 40-year lease on the 17,000 acres. Of that immense tract the Rogers Brothers and Crescent Coal companies of Greenville now own the Buell holdings and mineral rights of several thousand acres of the Alexander estate.

Buell's plans of becoming a coal baron were disrupted and finally dissipated. Green River was leased by the Green and Barren River Navigation Company, and freight rates raised to freeze out Buell. The owners of the river controlled the shipments of coal. Buell fought them with his old-time determination, and finally in 1888 the Federal government took over the river. But that was too late for the General, who died ten years later. He eked out an existence on the farm during the long-drawn-out litigation until a political appointment at Louisville made easier his declining years. The Airdrie of Alexander's dreams failed before operations were really underway, because the man heading the enterprise tired of the primitive life and returned to the pleasure of breeding race horses and living the life of a Bluegrass gentleman. And the Airdrie of Buell gradually passed out of existence because the old soldier was not equipped to fight with weapons used by financiers.

Now Hard to Reach

To reach Airdrie now the visitor goes either by way of Paradise or Rockport. The site is on the river between. A rutted trail, hard to negotiate by automobile, winds through scrubby timber, second growth, across a barren field, and the vicinity of the once promising industrial city is reached before the stranger is aware. A guide points out the places of interest where Alexander's immigrants built their homes, and where openings were made for iron and then coal mines. The ruins are nearby without warning. A veritable jungle hides the few remaining units of the once ambitious scheme. A winding path, shadowed by bulging rocks, points toward the river which is hidden by timber. Then the massive stone fence along side the ledge below which rears the tall crest of the blast furnace and power house reached by stone steps. Such fine examples of masonry are now found only in the finished works of modern artisans. All is gone except these stable but small parts of the comprehensive industrial plan. Fire destroyed the Buell house in 1907, and gradually, the other buildings were burned or crumbled into decay. The general's stepdaughter, Miss Nannie Mason, sold the farm and died in Louisville, following the death of the General at Airdrie.

Strangely misnamed was this little river town, if those who first called it Paradise hoped for permanence, for with the end of transport afloat, it rapidly declined and the Paradise of today is a gaunt reminder of the thriving trading point in Alexander's and Buell's days. And while there is about it a feeling of peace, it was the near setting for a glaring paradox in the buoyant hopes of the Scottish immigrants and later the associates of Buell. It was the chosen spot for the planting of two vigorous dreams of industrial supremacy.

(Editor's note: Little did the writer know that in just 30 years after this article was first published, that this little community of Paradise would be entirely obliterated as a town from both the face of the earth and from all maps, in favor of the vast Paradise TVA Steam Plant.)

Both the founder of the potential iron foundry headquarters and his successor were men who visioned vast projects without the faculty of building, and as the reign of Alexander ended in abandonment after spending $350,000 so were the years of the former Federal general climaxed by failure. And the once promising village hard by Paradise perished after a season of glamour under both masters, the stone wall, the lofty flights of steps and the blast furnace and the power house standing like determined sentinels toward the memories of departed grandeur and thwarted ambition. For fame was both alluring and elusive to General Don Carlos Buell, who rode the crest of favoritism for a while, which mocked him when his laurels turned to ashes of disillusionment and disappointment. A visit to Airdrie is worth the exertion. It leads the stranger over rugged terrain, an abandoned town site and beside the placid river. The muse of history oft pauses, for those who love to re-explore a territory once vibrant with life, and when the hills are clothed in moonlight, fancy may easily people them again. It is a chapter of which many know little, though they live nearby.

Ruins of Old Airdrie Furnace

Reminder of Little Bit o' Scotland

Sam Smith of Paradise Tells About It

From the *Evansville Press,* August 8, 1937

Paradise, Ky. — The natives of this section of western Kentucky all speak in the traditional soft southern drawl.

But there was a time when a goodly percentage of residents talked with the burr of the Scots.

That was when the town of Airdrie existed.

Paradise, Ky., was settled in 1792. Airdrie, Ky., sprouted up a quarter-mile from Paradise on the banks of Green River in 1855. It died in 1868. General Don Carlos Buell of Civil War fame was responsible for its death.

The General didn't enter the picture of Airdrie, Ky., at first.

Before him came Robert and Charles Alexander, a canny pair of Scots whose original home was in Lanark Shire's municipal police burgh in Airdrie (Scotland).

* * *

Airdrie, Scotland, which lies not far from Glasgow, was just a market town in the late sixteen hundreds. Its prosperity came when great coal and iron beds were found in the vicinity. With the discovery, naturally came brass and iron foundries.

So Robert and Charles Alexander knew all the "ins and outs" of handling iron from the raw to finished material when they set sail to America.

When the survey made by the celebrated David Dale Owen of New Harmony, Ind., first U. S. geologist, indicated that Kentucky was rich with iron ore deposits, the Alexanders were among the first to attempt to develop the fields.

Aided by foreign capital they built what was then considered the largest iron furnace in the country. Its ruins still stand — one of the few monuments left of this western Kentucky industry.

* * *

About this furnace, a primitive open-top affair some 75 feet high, grew a good sized town. At one time it had a population of around 180. There were several stores, a blacksmith shop and machine shop. There were two hotels — one of 48 rooms and the Torrence House with 14 rooms.

This was the Airdrie, Ky., that General Buell saw during the Civil War. Buell visited the town while his army and that of General Bragg were see-sawing across Kentucky.

* * *

Sam Smith, 60-year-old resident of Paradise, said the general liked the place and was impressed with the possibility of developing the iron ore industry.

"He came back to Airdrie in 1868, after the war closed," Mr. Smith said.

"Buell took over the 17,000 acres of coal and iron ore land from the Alexanders. He operated the furnace just three days and then shut it down.

"It was never reopened."

A clue as to why General Buell cut short the life of the iron furnace is contained in some of the earlier western Kentucky histories.

The Alexanders had been trying to use raw coal for fuel in their iron furnaces. This, coupled with the fact that knowledge in those days did not extend to a practical method of removing impurities from the ore, made the pig iron produced by the Airdrie furnace a low grade product.

* * *

General Buell tried substituting coke for raw coal in the furnace. His employees spent weeks manufacturing enough coke to operate the big smelter. But the first heat proved unsuccessful and Buell shut down the furnace.

Sam Smith says that after that the rumor got started that General Buell planned to "run out" the coal on his 17,000-acre property, and that by the time his lease had expired, all the coal about Airdrie, Ky., would be worked out.

"The Alexanders feared that Buell would actually carry out the plan," Mr. Smith said. "They negotiated with him to regain possession of the coal lands.

"In exchange for them, the Civil War general was given a 1000-acre estate bordering Green River in addition to the town of Airdrie."

* * *

All this happened years ago. Today the town of Airdrie doesn't exist. The passing years have blended the coal lands and the town into one. It serves as a sort of unofficial park for this section of western Kentucky.

Airdrie today is nothing but a few rough stones that mark the place where a fireplace stood, where there was a brick walk, where the foundation of an old store was located.

"The buildings were all torn down or just rotted away," Mr. Smith said.

"A few of them were moved to Paradise.

"I can remember when most of them were still here. Airdrie was a favorite spot for the boys around here to play. Why, I was almost 16 before I knew there were other people in the world besides Scotchmen," he said with a laugh.

"Some of the descendants of the iron workers brought from Scotland still live around here."

The 3,000-foot shaft into the side of Green River's cliffs where the Alexanders slope-mined their coal as well as iron ore still yawns blackly.

Picnickers use it for shelter during rains. There has been many a wiener-roast fire built in its mouth.

* * *

The massive stone powerhouse for the furnace is still there, too.

Tradition has it that it once served as a Civil War prison. Sam Smith says it didn't.

"Years ago, when Eddyville, Ky., prison was being built, a number of convicts were shipped to Airdrie," he said. "They were housed in the old powerhouse for a few weeks. They were sent here to quarry out some blocks of stone to be tested for use in building the penitentiary.

"Officials decided against using the Green River stone. Three or four big blocks that they quarried still lie on the river bank.

"While prison officials didn't like the stone, railroad men did. Piers for the old Evansville-Henderson L&N bridge were built of stone quarried at Airdrie."

Outlines of the big sand pit into which the iron was allowed to run from the blast furnace and cool into "pigs" can still be traced. So can the big reservoir that held water for the power plant.

* * *

Scattered through the brush and scrub trees that have grown up about the furnace can be found pieces of coke that were used to fire the big furnace.

"When the plant was shut down there were some 10,000 tons of coke stored here," Mr. Smith recalled. "It all burned."

Mr. Smith remembers General Buell and his stepdaughter, Miss Nancy Mason, who continued to live in the Buell home after the general's death in 1898.

"The General was a real old southern general gentleman despite the fact that he served on the Union side," he said.

"He spent a fortune in improving his estate..

"You can still follow the miles of woodland walks he constructed. They were all surfaced with this red ore slag.

"The General built bridges just so he could build bridges. Every little gully in the place was bridged several times with stone.

"His home was beautiful. It contained 19 to 20 rooms. There was a huge porch across the front facing the river."

* * *

All that is left of the Buell home is a few fire-blackened rotting timbers. It burned 22 years ago. Smith said the fire started from hot coal ashes dumped at the edge of a back porch by a shiftless servant.

The estate was later bought by the Five-J Coal Company. It is now owned by Crescent and Rogers Coal Company.

Gateway and steps to the Green River from the Buell home.

Paradise residents hope that some day the estate will be taken over by the Commonwealth and converted into a park."

AIRDRIE

Area Iron Works
Of Historical Interest

By Chuck Poehlein
Owensboro, Ky. *Messenger/Inquirer*, December 8,
1968

This year, by act of Congress, the Saugus Iron Works in Massachusetts was designated a national historic site.

The authentic restoration and reconstruction of the 17th century birthplace of a great industry was based on research of archaeologists and historians and was accomplished largely through private donations.

In a similar vein, an iron works built in the mid-1800s near Paradise, in Muhlenberg County (Ky.), represents a page out of economic and social history of our nation.

Though it was an economic failure, the iron foundry nonetheless is a fine example of 19th century ingenuity and skill in the arts of stone dressing and construction and is a physical reminder of the pioneer spirit which contributed to this nation's development.

The fortresss-like stone machinery house and 50-foot high smelting furnace of the Airdrie Iron Works are deteriorating now, yet still show clearly the skill and precision of the artisans who built them in 1855.

It's the hope of some local historians and naturalists that Airdrie can somehow be preserved from destruction by strip mining operations being carried on near the site.

Grounds on which the pre-Civil War foundry is located are owned by the Pittsburgh and Midway Coal Co., presently mining coal a few hundred yards from a bluff overlooking Airdrie.

A spokesman for the company said that mining officials do no have any definite plans concerning the foundry but that the situation would be discussed with representatives at the company's home in Missouri.

The history of Airdrie began in 1820 when William D. McLean opened a coal mine which became known as the McLean Drift Bank below Paradise. He was one of the first men to report the existence of coal in Western Kentucky and also one of the first to recognize the coal of Muhlenberg County as a desirable fuel. During the 1830s, McLean operated the mine and barged coal down the Green River to southern markets.

A geological survey was conducted in 1851 by Alexander (Scotch) Hendrie, and it was believed that coal and iron ore existed in the area in quantity and quality enough to make the production of iron a profitable venture.

A Scotchman, Robert Sproul Crawford Aitcheson Alexander, who resided in Woodford County, near Versailles, Ky., became interested in the mining prospects.

Alexander was born in Frankfort, Ky., and educated in Scotland. His family controlled an iron smelting industry in Scotland, and when their supply of iron ore began to run low, he decided to move the operation to Kentucky. Believing that the Scots were the best iron men in the world, Alexander, it is reported, imported 26 Scottish families to start and operate his new iron industry.

The Scots arrived at the site of the proposed foundry in 1855 and set about clearing the land, quarrying stone, building the foundry and homes and mining coal from the McLean Drift Mine.

The town of Airdrie included houses, a hotel and a company store and overlooked the iron works and the mines. Only broken pottery and bottle glass remain today at the town site. A fire destroyed most of the structures in the early 1900s, and weathering has eroded all other traces of urban life.

After costing its sponsors more than $250,000, Alexander closed the furnace in 1855 as precipitously as he had started it after only three "runs".

Several theories have evolved to explain the reason for abandoning the smelting operations. One is that the iron ore was not of desirable quality as previously supposed; another is that impurities in the local ore were different from those found at the Scottish sites; and a third is that management would not adopt methods to make the project profitable.

Historians report that Alexander was said to be by far the richest man in Kentucky at the time, and the money he lost at Airdrie was just "a drop in the bucket".

No further activity occurred at Airdrie until 1865 when Don Carlos Buell, a Union general, arrived on the scene. Buell, forming the Airdrie Petroleum Co., leased for 40 years the 12,778 acre tract and gave 56,875 shares of the capital stock to Alexander for the right to drill for oil, work fire clay and mine coal. Finding no oil after nine borings, Buell petitioned the legislature to amend the charter and change the name to Airdrie Coal and Iron Co., in December, 1865. Buell spent the next 33 years of his life there until his death in 1898. His efforts were directed to mining coal which he shipped to southern markets on barges.

As the years passed, legends have built up around Airdrie. Stories of prisoners in chains working the coal mine, of the stone machinery house serving as a prison for prisoners during the Civil War, and the tale that the stone house was built by and for state convicts, appear today to have no basis in fact.

The truth is that about the year 1884, Buell housed about 15 prisoners there to quarry stone for the Eddyville prison, then under construction. Remaining there only a few weeks, the prisoners were returned to the prison when another stone source was discovered near Eddyville.

It is the wish of Owensboro's Tim Repko Chapter of the Kentucky Young Historians to initiate a drive to preserve, restore and utilize the buildings and grounds of the Airdrie Iron Foundry, "as a vital piece of real estate symbolizing the state's industrial history".

The chapter would like to ". . . establish (the area) as a park with either private or public funds, create a museum to be developed around the industrial theme, and use the facilities for conventions, meetings and related historical and heritage activities for the Young Historians and other state historical societies".

The Airdrie Iron Works is too valuable historically to allow destruction by man or further ruin by nature, they believe. A cooperative effort on the part of the Pittsburgh and Midway Coal Co., the Young Historians and other civic groups, and the Department of Wildlife and Conservation could perhaps result in a workable plan to preserve the foundry on equal merit with the Saugus Iron Works as a national historic site, they believe.

A sketch of the Airdrie stack by Robert A. Powell

Text and drawing by Kentucky Heritage Artist

AIRDRIE

Robert A. Powell
(Sebree Banner, September 1, 1977)

This vine-covered furnace stack stands among cedars and sycamores on a narrow strip of land between Green River and the hill upon which the town of Airdrie was built.

Near the village of Paradise on the banks of the river, 12 miles northeast of Greenville, Sir Robert Alexander erected this stack in 1855. A Kentucky-born descendant of a titled Scottish family, Alexander purchased 17,000 acres of land lying along Green River where a large deposit of iron ore had been discovered.

He was born in Frankfort in 1819 and was educated in Scotland. He brought from Scotland a number of miners and furnace men to help develop the area. They built an iron furnace, a mill, a large stone house, a hotel, and a number of houses for the iron workers. The cylindrical iron-shell stack, 50 feet high, rests on a 26-foot-square stone base, 20 feet high. Nearby, they constructed an old, fort-like, three-story sandstone building to house the machinery for the furnace blast and rolling mills.

Shaded by trees and covered with Virginia Creeper are 60 stone steps on the site of the "Alexander House", destroyed by fire in 1907.

Several attempts to run the furnace were unsuccessful. The Scottish workmen were unfamiliar with Kentucky metallurgical practices; the ore required different treatment from that found in Scotland. After spending more than $300,000 without producing a pound of salable iron, "Lord Alexander" abandoned the project and retired to a large Bluegrass farm he had purchased in Woodford County.

The town of Airdrie was named for Alexander's Scottish home.

In 1866, General Don Carlos Buell bought 1,000 acres of the land, including the Airdrie furnace, to prospect for oil. He found more coal and iron than oil and attempted to work those deposits. Freight rates were so high the venture was not profitable, and he, too, abandoned the works. Buell lived here until his death in 1898.

Today, only this ancient stack marks the site of short-lived Airdrie.

Views of the rustic old foot bridges in General Buell's private park at Airdrie. These pictures are from newspaper clippings.

The Scots of Airdrie

The Legends of Airdrie tell that Sir Robert S. C. A. Alexander created Airdrie totally through the work of Scottish immigrants — those he "imported" by invitation only from the Airdrie district of Scotland.

But truth is unerring. The truth is that while Alexander's hand-picked Scots were in the vast majority in that tiny army of men which brought the village, the furnace and the Stone House up from bare ground, there were a number of talented and well-educated Englishmen who were much in evidence also during the construction and brief operation at Airdrie.

These include the Roll (Roole) family, many of them Kentucky-born, who were early on hand in the Airdrie community, along with the families of **Francis (Frank) Toll** and **Robert Kipling**, the pattern maker, all of English descent.

And then there were the native Muhlenberg County stone masons, **Alfred Johnson** and his son, **Lonz Johnson**; and **Thomas Sumner** and his son, **Alney McLean Sumner**. Without their masonry skills, the furnace and stone works may have never been completed. At least not in such fine and lasting fashion.

Also take into consideration that not all the Scotsmen who came to Airdrie, Kentucky, came directly from Airdrie, Scotland, at Alexander's beckon. Some of the more influential ones, namely the Pollacks and the Duncans were already in America — in Pennsylvania — when they received the invitation of Alexander to join him in this venture.

Regardless of all of this, Airdrie in Muhlenberg County was still a true Scottish community — then, and even today, the Scottish influences can still be felt strongly among their succeeding generations.

Names such as Hendrie, Patterson, Duncan, Heath, McDougal, Sneddon, Wilson, Keith, Williamson, Hamilton, Torrence, Robertson, Pennman, Muir, Campbell, Main and Gilmore dot the history of the area. Their names appear on deeds, court records, school censuses, church rolls and other forms of documents which go toward the make up of history. The blood of many of these still flows in the veins of fourth, fifth and sixth generations of Muhlenberg County residents. And proudly does it flow in both the minds and the eyes of these descendants.

At most, at any one time, no more than sixty Scottish-born citizens lived in Muhlenberg County — the most of whom were congregated in the Airdrie community. The 1860 census of Muhlenberg County reflects these families.

- **Gilbert Muir**, 44, an engineer, born in Scotland, with his wife, Agness T., 43 and children, Jane N., 21; Agnes, 11, James 8, and John, 6.

- **William Hamilton**, 54, a miner, Scotland; wife, Isabelle, 54; children, Elizabeth, 14, Catherine, 11, William, 9, Wallace, 4, and Isabelle, 2. All the children save the latter two were born in Scotland. Wallace was born in 1856 in Pennsylvania and Isabelle in 1858 in Kentucky.

- **Alexander Morris**, 35, a millwright, Scotland; wife, Mary, 37; children, Thomas H., 8, Margaret, 5, Alex, 13 (said to have been born in Kentucky). Thomas was born in Scotland and Margaret in Kentucky.

- **Alexander Campbell**, 26, miner, Scotland; wife, Agnes M., 20, Scotland; children, George E., 2, Scotland and

William, 1, Kentucky.

- **John Main**, 36, miner, Scotland; wife, Jenetta A. (Pollack), 24, Scotland; children, Mary, 4, Kentucky; Archibald, 2, Kentucky and Sally, 3 months, Kentucky. *(For further information on this family, see Tales of the Bicentennial).*

- **James Gilmore** (Gilmour), 32, miner, Scotland; wife, Jane, 21, Scotland; children, Agnes, 2, born in Kentucky and Matthew, two months. also born in Kentucky.

- **Robert Campbell**, 21, miner, Scotland; wife, Catherine, 18, Scotland; child, George, one month old, born in Kentucky.

- **John McDougle** (McDougal), 38, miner, Scotland; wife, Jane, 39, Scotland; children, Mary, 15, Jane, 11, and William, 9, all born in Scotland; Agnes, 6, born in Pennsylvania, and Ann, 3, born in Kentucky.

- **Alexander Wilson**, 36, miner/tavern keeper, Scotland; wife, Jane G., 31, Scotland; children, Alexander, 7, and James, 5, Scotland; William, eight months, Kentucky.

- **Andrew Duncan**, 28, miner, Scotland; wife, Mary, 27, Scotland; children, William, 8, and Mary, 7, Scotland; David, 5, Pennsylvania; Jane, 3, and Andrew, seven months, Kentucky.

- **Robert Duncan**, 24, miner, Scotland; wife, Mary, 24, Scotland; David, one, Pennsylvania.

- **David Duncan**, 18, Scotland.(Apparently unmarried.)

- **Willliam D. Pennman**, 22, miner, Scotland; wife, Annie, 16, France. They were living in the home of Francis Toll.

- **George Johnson**, 26, miner, England; wife, Jane R., 21, Scotland; Jane J., two months old, Kentucky. Also in this home were James Robertson, 20, a miner from Scotland; Joseph Robertson, 17, born on the Atlantic?

and Joseph Robertson, 8, born in Scotland.

- **William Esbitt** (Espy?), 32, miner, Ireland; wife, Rachel, 30, Scotland; Ellen, 10 and Martha, 9, born in Scotland and John, 7 and Ann 4, born in Virginia.
- **James Robertson**, 40, miner, Scotland, living in the home of William Gates.

In Greenville, Scottish born **Alexander Hendra** (Hendrie), 39, a carpenter lived with his family. Also in Greenville, **William A. Patterson**, 23, born in Scotland, was a college teacher.

At Mud River, **Robert Monroe**, 40, a miner born in Scotland, lived in the home of **Leander Penrod** and apparently worked in the Mud River Mine.

In the Central City-Kincheloe Bluff-South Carrollton area, two other Scottish-born miners lived with their families. **John Williamson**, was 30 and a coal miner. His wife, Mary J., 33, was also born in Scotland. Children William, 12, and Mary, 10, were likewise born in Scotland. Other children included John, 6, born in Ohio and Archibald, 4, and Robert, 1, born in Kentucky. In the home also was **Alexander McAlpin**, 34, a miner from Scotland.

In the same general area, the 1870 census showed **John Polake** (Pollack), 37, and his wife, Charlotte. John, a miner was born in Scotland and Charlotte, 22, in England. Children included Ann, 2, born in Pennsylvania. Next door, lived **Mary Polake**, 37, born in Scotland; her sons, Robert, 17, a miner, and Arch, 4, both born in Scotland. The census taker also listed Charlotte in this home also, but noted this was in error. All of these Pollacks descend from the original immigrant Archibald Pollack.

Of the English families listed at Airdrie, the names Vanlandingham, Roll (Roole), Kipling, Siddle and Toll are the most prevalent.

The Roll family, though of English descent, had been in America for many years since all listed in the 1860 census indicated they were born in Kentucky. Even the eldest, **Greenberry Roll**, 67, of the Paradise area, listed Kentucky as his birthplace.

The same is true of the Vanlandingham family, though the eldest, **O. C.** (Oliver Cromwell?) **Vanlandingham** is listed in the census as having been born in Louisiana. Others in the same family list Kentucky as their place of birth.

Francis (Frank) Toll, 46, of England, was prominent in the Airdrie area. He was a miner. Among his family were his wife, Ann, 40, also born in England; their sons, Richard P., 3, and Francis J., 2, both born in Kentucky. This family still has descendants living in Muhlenberg County.

The **Robert Kipling** family also enjoys a long line of descendants still residing in this area. **Robert Kipling** is erroneously listed in the 1860 census as "Robert Tiplin". However, the 1870 census lists him and his family correctly. Coming from England as a carpenter and pattern maker, Kipling, 32, and his wife, Rhoda (Roda), 33, had three children at the time. Precilla (Priscilla?), 7, and Eveline, 5, were born in England, and Madgaline, 1, was born in Kentucky. Also in the home were the only Roole (Roll) listed as born in England. She was **Nancy A. Roole**, 4. In the home also was a **Peggy Siddle**, 74, listed as born in England.

Interesting to note that in the 1870 census, a **Margaret Kipling**, 66, is listed as a housekeeper in the Paradise area, and was censused as being English by birth. Nearby, Robert, now 43, and his wife, Rhoda, 44, lived with their children, Precilla, Eveline, Madgaline, plus the additions of Henry,8, Rhoda (Roda), 8, George S, 7, Barbara E, 5, and Mary E., 2, born since the 1860 census was taken.

Possibly, Margaret was Robert's mother, who had come to Kentucky from England, following her son to this area. Other such English miners in the area of Airdrie-Paradise, were **Robert Blackburn** and **J. C. Thompson**. By 1870, Airdrie had been closed a dozen or more years. The population of the Scottish-born miners had begun to dissipate..

Many of the miners had gone to other areas seeking work. They followed the Duncans to McHenry in Ohio County. Some went to Aberdeen and Mining City in Butler County. Others found employment in the other coal mines of Muhlenberg County. Yet, as time passed, many of them returned to their first roots in Muhlenberg County and, as earlier noted, became useful and respected citizens in the community.

Among those still in the Airdrie-Paradise area in 1870 were **Nancy McGrath**, widow of Irish-born **Richard McGrath**; **John Pollack, J. D. Gregory**, a rock mason, **Arch Pollack, William Williamson, William Keith**, a carpenter, **John McDougal, David Duncan** and **James Gilmore**.

John Main remained in the county for a short time but soon moved on to Ohio County and later to Butler County. His family name, however, eventually disappeared from the list of citizens over the entire area, although some descendants by other surnames may still be found.

Andrew Duncan still lived in the county in 1870 and was soon instrumental in developing the vast W. G. Duncan Coal Company.

Both Duncan and Main were residents of the Paradise area in 1870. **William Pennman** also remained in Paradise for a while and mined coal.

John McLish was at Mud River as a miner.

Later census records show the families coming and going, moving from coal town to coal town — basically living out their lives in Muhlenberg, Butler and Ohio Counties where they continued to ply their trade as underground miners.

Families such as the Pollacks and the Duncans, as well as the Williamsons and Gilmores, are well remembered over a series of generations. Others have all but been forgotten.

However, the Scottish influence on that small corner of Muhlenberg County known as Paradise Country — and especially Airdrie on Green River — can never be erased from the history of this area nor from the minds of the many people who have heard over and over the tales of Airdrie which are now also contained within the walls of this booklet.

(Bobby Anderson)

An Historic Furnace: Airdrie

(This article, written by Cherie E. Sanders, then a student at Todd County Central High School in Elkton, Ky., first appeared in print in the Kentucky Heritage magazine in the Winter of 1969. Cherie is the daughter of Muhlenberg County, Ky., native and former Paradise resident Mattie Knight Sanders. Cherie grew up in the knowledge of the historical significance of Airdrie, having visited there annually with her family since her childhood, while reveling in the family lore of the Airdrie-Paradise area. The article was submitted by her mother for publication in this booklet.)

* * *

By CHERIE E. SANDERS SHEMWELL

Airdrie and its furnace were built in 1855 by R. S. C. A. Alexander, and since that time it has been one of the most interesting spots along Green River. General Don Carlos Buell made it his home in 1866 and continued to live there until his death in 1898. In the course of the years, Airdrie's twenty-five or more frame houses have all been abandoned. The deserted village became a demolished village, and today little is left to mark the site of this once flourishing town. No trace of the buildings that stood on Airdrie Hill can now be found. Some of the houses were carried off in the shape of lumber; other tumbled down years ago and rotted away.

The Buell residence, erected by William McLean many years before Airdrie was started, was not only the largest and oldest residence in this place but was also the last to

99

pass away. It burned in 1907. This historic mansion stood in a beautiful park near the top of Airdrie Hill on which the town was built. Now it is just a windswept hillside about a mile from Paradise, Kentucky. Today, not a trace of the town remains.

However, the ruins of Airdrie Furnace remain remarkably well-preserved. On the narrow strip of land between the water's edge and the top of the hill, and running parallel with the river, are now found the only evidences of the old iron works and the old mines. Here and there, protruding from the ground, can be seen traces of old stone walls that remind one more of the work of prehistoric mound-builders than of a foundation laid by mill-builders. Two of the old shafts look like long-abandoned wells, and another like a mere hole in the ground. The opening on the hillside, leading into the abandoned drift mine, known as "McLean Old Bank", looks like the entrance to a cave that has never been explored.

The stack of the furnace still stands, a majestic old pile, fifty-five feet or more in height. Near the stack is the stone house, possibly able to defy storm and sunshine for many years to come. This house, used in former times for machinery, is a sandstone structure three stories high, fifty by twenty feet. The wooden floors and window frames have long ago fallen away. This fort-like building was at one time covered with a slate roof which was ruined by visitors throwing rocks on it from the top of the bluff at the foot of which the house stands. About half-way up the wall of the stone house, between the large windows, the thoughtful architect placed a large stone bearing the inscription "AIRDRIE, 1855".

The hillside stone steps leading from a point just beyond the stone house to the top of Airdrie Hill, where the town stood, are most picturesque. Virginia creeper has found its way up the solid stone foundation, along with moss and clusters of clinging ferns. The sixty stone steps, although without railing, can still be climbed in safety.

Airdrie Venture Cost One Third of A Million Dollars

Airdrie was built in 1855 by Sir R. S. C. A. Alexander who invested more than a third of a million dollars in the undertaking before calling it quits. That's a fortune today and an unbelievable amount of money 110 years ago.

The Airdrie operation involved some 17,000 acres in Muhlenberg County. Sir Alexander named the furnace and the town after Airdrie, Scotland, which is about midway between Edinburgh and Glasgow and the seat of Alexander's title and estate.

Sir Alexander, also known as Lord Alexander, was born in Frankfort, Kentucky in 1819, but removed to Scotland to become heir to land, fortune and a title.

Dwindling iron ore reserves in Scotland caused Sir Alexander to look for a new source of supply. He settled upon the ore found along the Green River. Sir R. S. C. A. Alexander (whose name was Robert Sproul Crawford Atcheson Alexander) bought 17,000 acres in Muhlenberg County to start operation.

Alexander believed the Scotch were the most competent iron workers in the world, and so, during the latter part of 1854, he brought many of his former employees and their families to the new Airdrie. A special ship, it is said, was chartered for this trip. It required six weeks for their sailing vessel to cross the ocean. Tradition has it that their boat had a collision with a water-logged boat, which resulted in changing their course to such an extent that they landed in New York instead of Philadelphia. From Pittsburgh they came down the Ohio, and after some delay in Louisville, Kentucky, they started up the Green River. Upon arriving in Airdrie, their "New Scotland", they immediately set to work finishing the houses begun in the new town by Alexander Hendrie. This group from Scotland included masons, carpenters, and miners, metal workers and furnace tenders; they built a town and an industry in 1855.

Furnace Starts, Fails

After considerable drilling, digging and delaying, the furnace was finally started. Alexander, as I have said before, believed the Scotch were the most competent iron workers in the world, and he gave them full sway. While his men may have been thoroughly familiar with the handling of the Black Band ore of Scotland, they evidently did not realize that the ore here required a different treatment. Three or four unsuccessful attempts were made to run the furnace. The trouble lay not on the ore, but on the management. Had they changed some of their methods, the probabilities are that the undertaking would have been a grand success.

Airdrie's days of ascent were numbered. The work of the masons was sound, but the industrial plans of Sir Alexander were not.

Alexander had calculated to use the coal raw in the furnace instead of converting it to coke. The result, according to history, was a product low in quality and short in quantity. Shortly after the furnace began operation, a flywheel broke and forced a shutdown. This was repaired but there was another mechanical breakdown.

After the second breakdown, Sir Alexander lost his patience and gave up. The furnace was never charged again. The superintendent of the furnace had already made plans to switch to coke, but these plans were never carried out.

In all, the furnace was not in blast more than six weeks to two months. The men were discharged and the furnace was closed. While this was the end of the industry, the community continued.

The Scots brought here by Alexander brought new blood to Muhlenberg County. Many of the names survive and are now an inextricable part of western Kentucky heritage. One was my own great-great-grandfather, Robert Kipling, the patternmaker, who was from Durham, England. After the works were abandoned, he located on a farm near Paradise, where he died March 10, 1902. He designed and cast a number of door props called "Old Jack Robertsons." They were iron figures about ten inches wide and five inches high, representing "Old Jack" sitting on the floor with his legs stretched out, a goose between them, and he in the act of carving it. A few of these iron door weights can still be found in the county.

The Buell Era

Airdrie is famous for another reason. After the Civil War, Don Carlos Buell — the Union Army general who save Grant's army from defeat at Shiloh — retired to Airdrie. Immediately after the close of the war General Buell began a search for an oil field. He came to Airdrie from Marietta, Ohio, in 1866 for the sole purpose of working the oil on the Alexander lands.

He took a forty-year mineral and oil lease on the Alexander 17,000 acres. The company,

Above the old Airdrie stone house in 1934, picking blackberries, Laura M. Knight, Nell Markham, Laura Evelyn Knight and Mattie E. Knight.

The stone house and stack (background) at Airdrie, left; and below, the author of the ensuing article, Cherie Sanders and Howard Shemwell on Airdrie's sixty steps.

Photos Courtesy
Mattie Knight Sanders
and
Cherie Sanders Shemwell

of which General Buell was president, was known as Airdrie Petroleum Company.

Buell drilled extensively on the Alexander property along Green River. Airdrie being on the Green River and having the best transportation facilities, he decided to establish himself there. Furthermore, after the death of Alexander, heirs wishing to dispose of some of the property which they had inherited entered into an agreement with Buell. Buell received a deed to the Airdrie furnace and about a thousand acres around it for having released the forty-year lease that he held. He therefore confined his work to his own property near Airdrie. However, the coal Buell discovered while looking for oil was in such abundance that he changed his plans and directed most of his attention to coal development.

General Buell lived in the house once owned by Sir Alexander for thirty-two years, including four years (1885-1889) he made Louisville his headquarters while Pension Agent of Kentucky. In 1883 and during a number of years following, he was one of its early members of the Kentucky State Agricultural Society and was also identified with many conventions that have aided in the development of the resources of the State. In 1890, when the Shiloh Military Park Commission was organized, he was appointed one of the members and served on that board up to the time of his death. Although never an applicant for office, General Buell's name had been mentioned in connection with high offices, among them being the presidency of the United States.

Today, Airdrie is almost impossible to find by road and not even easy to locate by going downstream on the Green River.

Vegetation has made creeping but inevitable progress in obliterating the traces of man except for the stone work erected by the Scots. Portions of the Airdrie works appear as stable as the day they were built.

Ghost stories about Airdrie still persist. There are stories that Alexander used slaves, that Buell held captured Confederate soldiers as prisoners there, and that it once was a prison.

There's a kernel of truth in all of this. When the state penitentiary at Eddyville was enlarged in the early 1880s, a few convicts were brought to Airdrie to quarry stone. They were kept at the works.

While the ghost stories probably are without foundation, most any visitor there will tell you that you can stand at the top of the hill today and almost feel that pulse of a town that once lived.

Such, as I have tried to describe it, is the Airdrie of today (1969). Although Airdrie's history didn't begin until 1855, the traditions of the neighborhood go back to the end of the who opened up a farm and with his own sons, Jacob and Henry, conducted the first store where the landing is; and it is very probable that before their deaths, along in the 1840s, that the name of the settlement was changed (from Stum's Landing) to Paradise.

At Paradise, during the early 1960s, a new sound could be heard and signs of a new industry were evident. From Old Airdrie only the muffled sound of construction noises drifted the one mile down the Green River from Paradise, where the world's largest steam-electric power plant was going up. This seemed to break the long silence which hangs heavy over the once flourishing iron-making settlement of Airdrie. Indeed, the silence is a fitting requiem, for Airdrie is a ghost town.

On December 30, 1967, I visited Paradise, Kentucky, for a last look. This was the great day of Exodus. Everyone must evacuate.

The last Post Office & Buchanan's store, Paradise 1967.

As I looked down the main, and only, street of Paradise, I couldn't help but to think how right the papers were to call it Paradise Lost. The area was to become another stock pile for storage of coal for the world's largest steam plant, but I found no comfort in this.

My mind wandered again to nearby Airdrie, which stands as a monument for the graveyard that was once called Paradise. It was a fitting burial that it should be buried in "Black Coal."

AIRDRIE FURNACE

A Spectacular Failure

By DAVID KENNAMER
State News Bureau
The Leader-News, March 21, 1973

Frankfort, Ky. — Can you visualize Kentucky, an agricultural and industrial state, as a major iron center of America?

A century and a half ago, many Kentuckians may have argued that the state's future hinged on iron production.

By 1837 the state ranked third in the nation in iron production, and at one time there were more than 70 stone blast furnaces producing tons upon tons of iron.

The ruined furnaces now stand as mute witnesses to a fascinating period of Kentucky history.

Nearly all of these furnace sites have been identified in 23 counties spread throughout the state. Most important to Kentucky's iron age was the northeast corner of the state known as the Hanging Rock Iron Region which includes Greenup, Boyd, and Carter Counties; and Lyon and Trigg Counties in what is now the Land Between the Lakes Region. There are 15 furnaces and furnace sites marked in Greenup County alone.

The technology of the 19th century required vast amounts of charcoal to produce the high temperatures needed in the iron smelting process. A unique combination of shallow ore deposits, vast forests and navigable streams gave Kentucky its early advantage and opportunity.

The first furnace west of the Allegheny Mountains was built in Bath County near Owingsville in 1791. Designed to cast iron kettles, it was used to make cannon balls during the War of 1812. Today it is known as the Bourbon Iron Works.

The remains of furnaces in the Land Between the Lakes region have become major attractions. Center Furnace, the last charcoal-fired furnace to operate in Kentucky, was built in the 1840s and was used periodically for 65 years. This operation required the labor of 250 to 300 men who lived in the nearby community of Hematite. During this era, Chinese laborers were imported to work at this furnace and at others in the area.

At nearby Eddyville, William Kelly experimented at his Suwanee Iron Works and in 1847 discovered a method of making steel by forcing cold air into molten iron. In England, Henry Bessemer was doing this same thing. Kelly was granted a patent process in the United States, but Bessemer got the credit, the fame and the fortune that went with it.

Even during the iron industry's heydey, not every furnace was a roaring success. Perhaps the most spectacular failure was the Airdrie Furnace near Paradise in Muhlenberg County.

In 1855 Sir Robert Alexander spent over $300,000 to build the furnace, which he named after his home in Scotland. His Scottish workers could never make the furnace yield and, according to a nearby highway marker, it finally closed without producing a single pound of salable iron. The ruins of Alexander's furnace still stand on a bluff above Green River.

By 1860 the iron industry had begun to decline. The iron ores found in Kentucky were of generally poor quality and transportation was often a problem.

Because the manufacture of iron took such huge quantities of wood, vast areas of forest land were devastated; in the Land Between the Lakes area almost every tree over two inches was cut. At this rate it did not take long to eradicate the native forests and the fuel supply.

When large deposits of high quality ore were found near the Great Lakes, Kentucky's iron age came to a close.

The remains of Buffalo Furnace stand at the entrance to Greenbo Lake State Resort Park. Long range plans exist for its restoration but according to Richard Money, Assistant Director of Construction and Maintenance for the State Department of Parks, these plans are "very indefinite. There aren't many plans on the board now. Quite a bit of work is needed to restore it to its original condition."

Built to withstand tremendous heat and pressure, the iron furnaces deteriorate very slowly while standing idle. Col. George Chinn, Director of the Kentucky Historical Society, says, "They aren't like covered bridges that fall apart. They don't need a lot of maintenance."

A project completed last year by the Kentucky Historical Society, the (Kentucky) State Highway Department and the Armco Steel Company of Ashland has resulted in placement of highway markers at each known furnace site.

Most of the restoration and preservation work done on the furnaces is conducted by the Department of Highway Bourbon Furnace has been made the center of a roadside park, and several others are being maintained in similar settings.

Wallace Williamson III, president of the Big Sandy Valley Historical Society, says he is not aware of any other plans for preservation in Kentucky. He points out that actual rebuilding of the furnaces is a very formidable undertaking. "There are always people who want to restore a furnace to its original condition but they have no idea how much money it takes. The actual restoration of a furnace is an exceedingly expensive proposition.

Although Kentucky's mineral emphasis has shifted to coal, blast furnaces still operate in the state. These are large modern installations such as Armco's Amanda Furnace near Ashland. Iron is no longer mined in Kentucky, so these furnaces depend on ore from other areas. Kentucky's colorful iron era is reflected by the place names still in use around the state. Argillite, Hematite, and Pactolus are just a few of them. Iron Works Pike, built to

STONE HOUSE and smelting furnace at Airdrie. Often the Stone House was referred to as a prison.

transport iron from the Bourbon Iron Works to the Kentucky River at Frankfort, still carries traffic. Winding just north of Lexington, one of the states most populous and modern areas, it shows that history is always nearby for those who take a minute to look.

AIRDRIE:

A Look At Its Colorful Past

By LESLIE SHIVELY SMITH

The late Mrs. Leslie Shively Smith of Drakesboro was for many years a respected teacher in the Muhlenberg County school system and author of the book "A Black History".

* * *

A look into the colorful past of this Green River country brings back to life the Scottish settlement of Airdrie in Muhlenberg County, on Green River, about a mile below the village of Paradise.

Nothing remains of the once-flourishing Airdrie except the sturdy walls of a stone house, picturesque stone steps and wall, the crumbling stack of an old iron furnace and the entrance to an abandoned mine.

These landmarks are surrounded by an abundant growth of sycamore and cedar trees. The large trees are interspersed with a lush undergrowth of wild vines and other vegetation.

A dirt road leading toward Airdrie from Kentucky 176 soon becomes impassable except by foot. Then it winds through the woods until a small clearing is reached. This is the top of Airdrie Hill, and many years ago when this point commanded a beautiful view of Green River numerous houses stood there. Now the view down the sloping hillside leading to the river is shut off by the dense foliage which almost hides the prominent stone landmarks.

The inscription *AIRDRIE 1855* is boldly chiseled into the ancient walls of the sandstone house three stories high, about 50 feet long and 30 feet wide. Floors, doors and window frames, evidently made of wood, must have decayed and fallen away years ago. The roof is gone, too. These massive walls stand about 50 yards from the river, and they once housed machinery used in connection with the furnace and mining operations.

The hillside steps, made of large, solid stone slabs, are 60 in number. They lead from the top of Airdrie Hill, where the town stood, to a point near the stone house.

Close by stands the crumbling 50-foot-high stack of the old furnace. Its cylindrical portion rests on a 36-foot-square stone base that's 20 feet high. Great arches lead inside the base to the furnace itself.

The entrance to the abandoned mine is found below the smokestack. This tunnel goes straight back into Airdrie Hill for about 40 yards and then seems to turn left.

And what brought all of this to Muhlenberg County? Well, the story begins in 1851, when Robert S. C. A. Alexander, the Frankfort, Kentucky–born descendant of a wealthy titled Scotch family, purchased 17,000 acres of land in this area, where the existence of a desired iron ore had been discovered.

The Alexanders formerly lived in Airdrie, a small town near Edinburgh, in Scotland. In their native land, the family's wealth was based on ironworks. The American-born Alexander brought in iron workers from Scotland because he thought their experience would be useful in developing the Muhlenberg County area.

The Scots began arriving late in 1854 after a six-week crossing of the Atlantic in a chartered ship. Their frame houses and the stone structures were built in 1855 and 1856.

Several attempts were made to run the furnace, but all were unsuccessful, for it seems that this ore required a different treatment from that found in Scotland. The workmen evidently did not realize that.

This unfortunate venture was abandoned soon after the buildings were completed. Consequently, the town of Airdrie was short-lived and it wasn't many years before the houses, stores and the settlement's two-story hotel building were all in ruins. Alexander moved to Woodford County but many of the workers whom he had brought to America remained in Muhlenberg County. Many of today's Muhlenberg residents with Scotch names are their descendants.

General Don Carlos Buell, a Union commander in the Civil War, made his home at Airdrie from 1866 until his death in 1898. He acquired that part of the Alexander holdings where Airdrie is located, to seek oil. But he found, instead, coal in such great quantities that he changed his plans and developed the coal field.

The house he occupied — which also had been Alexander's residence while he was at Airdrie — was destroyed by fire nine years after General Buell's death.

OLD AIRDRIE;

-

A Link With the 19th Century

By GARY KULA

Owensboro Messenger-Inquirer, July 30. 1967

Almost fortress-like, the old stone structure stands on the banks of the Green River, guarding the crumbling furnace and the long unused mine.

Surrounded now by dense growth of vegetation and partly covered by creepers, the Airdrie Iron Works are part of an almost forgotten portion of Muhlenberg County history.

The iron works are located near Paradise, Kentucky, approximately one mile down river from the town.

Started in 1855 by Robert S. C. Aitcheson Alexander, a wealthy Kentuckian descended from titled Scotsmen, the project folded after two years of unsuccessful operation.

Alexander was born in Frankfort, Kentucky, and educated in Scotland. His family controlled an iron smelting industry in Scotland and, when their supply of iron ore began to run low, Alexander decided to move the operation to Kentucky. Believing the Scots were the best iron men in the world, Alexander imported approximately 25 Scottish families to start and operate his new iron business. Alexander's geologists discovered at the Green River site, a rich vein of iron ore, which they thought was similar to the type required by them in their method of smelting.

The group of Scots arrived at the site of the doomed operation in 1855 and set about constructing a smelting furnace and a large storage building called the Stone House. They then began mining coal from what is called the McLean Old Bank Mine. The settlement founded by the immigrants was named Airdrie after the Scottish town from which they came.

The town of Airdrie itself overlooked the iron works and the mine. No recognizable remnants of the town remain today, as fire destroyed most of the structures in the early 1900s. Most of the town was abandoned by 1897 and the Alexander mansion, later owned by General Don Carlos Buell, burned in 1907.

So ended the town.

The ill-fated mining-smelting venture folded after three or four attempts at producing iron. Most historians agree that the Scottish smelters did not know how to remove the impurities from the local ore, or they wouldn't adopt methods to make the project profitable. The operation folded just as the miners found a vein of high quality ore, but Alexander chose to discontinue operations anyway and retired to his estate in Lexington, where he gained a reputation as a one of the state's best horse breeders.

Altogether, it is estimated that Alexander sank $350,000 into the operation. He was reputed to be the richest man in the state at the time.

Some Muhlenberg Countians can tell you many stories about the still-standing Stone House. The most popular of the tales is that Alexander housed prisoners in the three-story stone structure and used them to work his mines. Others in the region say General Buell housed prisoners there, some maintaining these were ones he captured in the Civil War.

These tales seem to grow from an incident which occurred in 1884.

The state decided to enlarge the Eddyville prison at that time and had made arrangements to quarry stone on the property, which Buell then owned.

This massive Stone House and stack were built at Airdrie in 1855.

Fifteen prisoners were shipped from the penitentiary to Airdrie and were lodged in the Stone House. Meanwhile, the state had located suitable stone near Eddyville and the prisoners were shipped to the new quarry before removing any stone from the Airdrie site.

The site of the furnace, Stone House, and mine are rather hard to reach now. The easiest way probably would be to leave by boat from Paradise and travel one mile down river. Farthest downstream is the furnace, where the unsuccessful smelting was attempted.

The furnace and the stack rise approximately 50 feet into the air. Within ten yards on the upstream side of the furnace, and standing nearly as high is the Stone House.

Still bearing a stone with the date "1855", and with a cedar tree growing from a stone beam across the second story of the structure, the building appears of time fairly well, lacking only a roof, windows and doors. Just beyond the building are a set of sixty stone steps coming down the bluff which overlooks the structures. The steps lead to the former site of the Airdrie iron works.

Another 200 feet beyond the stone steps is the opening to the mine, looking very much like a cave rather than a man-constructed tunnel.

Along the line of the mine's tunnel are ventilation shafts. These still show remnants of stacks, which mining officials believe were used to help ventilate the mine. Fires were believed to have been built in the shafts, causing the mine tunnel to act as a flue and create an artificial draft in the mine.

The land adjoining the old iron works is presently being strip mined by Pittsburgh & Midway Coal. Co., a subsidiary of Gulf Oil. Company officials said that the ruins would be left in their present condition. Mining would in no way endanger the condition of the iron works, they indicated.

The viewer of the over-a-century-old relics of a by-gone era and an almost forgotten way-of-life sees some indication of what industry of the days was like and how it must have been to live in the era after the Civil War. In fact, the relics seem to take the viewer back even farther, following his imagination to picture any scene that will fit with the surroundings.

AIRDRIE:

A Muhlenberg Ghost

Furnace Ruins Are All That Remain
Of Scot's Brief Attempt to Smelt Ore

By MASON SMITH
Owensboro (Ky.) Messenger-Inquirer

July 19, 1978

Let me tell you a ghost story.

The story explains a phantom you see as you push through undergrowth near Green River in southern Muhlenberg County (Ky.). We're a mile north of the dead city of Paradise, and several hundred yards from a coal beltline and loading dock owned by Pittsburgh and Midway Mining Co.

There, through the burlap weave of trees and bush branches, you glimpse the shimmering of a stone building. Stepping through a break in the rock, we climb down a set of crumbling stone steps into the leafy-dark warmth of the river plateau.

We have found Airdrie, the now nearly-forgotten site of what could have been an important iron smelting industry in early Kentucky.

In the 1850s several hundred Scotsmen quickened the area with mining, building and trading along the river between Bowling Green and Louisville. Now only snakes live inside the castle-like furnace stack and machine house they left rising 30 to 40 feet out of the brush.

The Scots thought they had found a new homeland, complete with Black Band iron ore they knew from

Scotland. They found no Black Band, but low-grade Kentucky ore, no salty lochs, but the flowing Green, no lowlands of Scotland, but the badlands (as Jesse Stuart called them) of western Kentucky.

The adventure failed, not through lack of funds, but through lack of stubbornness.

A wealthy central Kentucky landowner of Scottish descent, Robert S. C. A. Alexander, began the operation around 1851, investing $350,000 in the venture. The furnace and mines were ready by 1854. Nothing happened.

Alexander fired up his furnace three or four times, but when the Muhlenberg ore proved different from the Scottish ore, he quit.

Otto Rothert in his *"History of Muhlenberg County"* says: "The furnace was not in blast altogether more than six weeks to two months. The trouble was not in the ore but in the management. Had they changed some of their methods the probabilities are that the undertaking would have been a grand success."

It wasn't.

Alexander sold the 17,000 acres he owned around Airdrie in 1857 (named incidentally, for the family's home city 15 miles from Glasgow, Scotland) and moved to Lexington to breed horses.

Alexander apparently produced better horse flesh than pig iron. He died in 1867 still a wealthy man.

Since then the land has belonged to a Civil War general, Don Carlos Buell, and to various coal companies. It now belongs to Pittsburgh and Midway, which stripped the area in 1969-70.

"We really don't have that many visitors," said Robert E. Brown, superintendent of P&M's Muhlenberg mines. "It's so hard to get to."

Modern visitors must drive in past the mine near the TVA Paradise Power Station and follow a dirt road long the belt line to the river. A fairly healthy hike awaits them up the riverbank to the site.

"It's snaky, mighty snaky," said Brown. "Of course a lot of people come in by the river that we never know about. You can see the stack from the river — just barely — if you know what you're looking for."

One visitor who came by river, folk singer John Prine, remembers the stack even though nearly 20 years have passed since he visited the site.

"I must have been 12 or 13 at the time," Prine said in a telephone interview from Nashville. "It was just a magical place to me. We had to lean down in the boat to get under the trees overhanging the bank. You couldn't get in by land then."

Prine mentioned Airdrie in his song about Paradise and Peabody Coal Co. that began, "*Daddy, won't you take me back to Muhlenberg County. . .*"

The lyrics refer to the "old prison on the Green" (or down by Airdrie Hill?) Tradition lingers that the stack once held convicts. Rothert says that story began in the 1880s when the state quartered a group of 15 prisoners in the stone machine house while they were quarrying stone. He says prisoners remained at Airdrie only a few weeks, however.

Mostly, the site has remained vacant. Later owners, including Buell, planned to smelt iron, using the furnace, the area's ore and the river.

Politics, more than chemistry, frustrated Buell. After the Civil War, Kentucky leased the river to a private company, the Green and Barren River Navigation Co., whose rates shut Buell out of the market.

By the time Buell broke the company's monopoly, time had broken Buell. He died in Alexander's riverside mansion (now completely gone) in 1896.

Over the years the house and the village rotted away, leaving only the stone skeleton of the furnace. Brown said P&M had no plans for the ruins. Other people, however, do have plans.

Dan Kidd, with the Kentucky Heritage Commission, said Airdrie will get "strong consideration" for nomination to the National Historic Register later this year.

"It's probably the top site in Muhlenberg County for nomination," Kidd said. He added the other top contender is the county courthouse in Greenville.

Kidd said being named to the national register makes available 50-50 matching grants for historic restoration, and brings a certain amount of protection from federally-funded construction projects.

"It doesn't affect the private owner too much unless he gets a grant," Kidd said. "Once he gets a grant there are strings attached to guarantee preservation for a certain number of years."

Kidd said Airdrie already appears on the state register, "But that's mostly honorary recognition," he added.

Aside from tolerating the ruins, Muhlenberg hasn't been overly hospitable to ghosts from a bygone era. It wasn't too hospitable to the living Alexander, whom friends called "The Lord" of the estate.

Rothert recorded an encounter between "Lord" Alexander and a Muhlenberg backwoodsman named Williams. Williams "sashayed" up to Alexander and said:

"So you are the Lord, are you? By gum you're nothing more but a human bein' after all and a plain ordinary, say-little sort of feller at that. They said you was a Big Bug, but five-foot-six will reach you any day of the week, by Washington!"

Alexander apparently laughed the meeting off and shook hands with Williams. With no ill-feelings or murders on the site, the Scotsman's ghost has found other halls to haunt.

AIRDRIE

Kentucky's Famous Deserted City

Two Escaped Prisoners Lost
Forever in Nearby Cave

*Legend: Robbers Cut Off Young Girl's Head
And Tossed It Into the Blazing Fireplace*

*(Editor's Note: This article first appeared in the
Louisville Courier-Journal on February 2, 1911, under the
title "Kentucky's Famous Old Deserted City". It re-
appeared in the Central City Times-Argus on January 28,
1960, after the original copy was resurrected by Alexander
(Sandy) Cather of Beech Creek. Much imagination was
written into this article by the original author, and much
more folklore than fact is woven into the story. The reader
is cautioned that all which appears here is not fact but an
outgrowth of the historic Legends of Airdrie. Indeed, much
of it should be read with tongue-in-cheek. The author is
unknown.)*

* * *

Far away from the strife and turmoil of the world, the
death-like silence which enshrouds it broken by cries of the
wild things that are monarchs of all they survey, there is
nestled in the hills along Green River, the remnants of a
once populous village. The houses are tumbled down with
the weight of the years and inattention, and the one-time
streets are overgrown with bushes, by grass, even a tall tree
occasionally rising itself to block progress. In every

direction is an almost complete wilderness and a few examples of man's handiwork, as a reminder that here, in the years long past, hardy pioneers sought to wrest wealth free from Mother Nature's storage place.

All of the subtle atmosphere of romance that envelops the abandoned cities of the old world abound in Airdrie; Airdrie, once destined to be the most thriving town in Western Kentucky. Here, a half-century ago, men built and delved into the earth and thrived in the fruits of their labors. Then transportation difficulties presented themselves and the wheels of industry were stilled. The giant machinery that once moved to the touch of the engineer's hand is now the meeting place of birds of the airs, and the silence too seldom shattered by the human voice — and then only when visitors go to gaze upon the beauty and grandeur of the picturesque scenery.

Airdrie is located on a rugged hill, rising some 250 feet above the old high water mark on the river's brink. Massive stone steps lead from the disused landing stage to the top of the hill, where stands the old smelter and prison, for 50 years ago offenders against the law were sent to Airdrie to expiate their misdeeds by working in the mines[4]. Beyond is the entrance to the mine shaft, the yawning mouth closed by a rotting plank and the dilapidated mine cars falling to pieces on the rails, just where they were left by the weary miners 50 years ago. Off in the distance through the tangled undergrowth, here may be seen the tumbled-down houses where lived the overseers and the officials of the company that founded the mine. Pursuing the dim tracery of a trail the wanderer who happens by this almost hidden village will see a somewhat larger, and if anything, more timeworn

---

[4] *Airdrie was not built as a prison, and was never actually used as a prison except to house a few state prisoners who were there while extracting stone to be used in the construction of the Eddyville prison. Prison labor and slave labor, otherwise, were never used at Airdrie. (Editor)*

building than the others. This is the old hotel, where in the halcyon days gathered many merry parties, where gaming for high stakes often took place, and where at least one cruel murder occurred if tradition is to be believed.

It is not necessary to be a sentimentalist and dreamer to sit under the arches of the forest and, in the imagination, picture the hilltop peopled with quaint figures of another day and time. Still less hard is it to gaze on the ruins of the once palatial mansion where for many years lived that famous old warrior, General Don Carlos Buell of Civil War fame, and in fancy see the peculiar old man, surrounded by a small army of servants and ruling like a king of the huge estate under his management.

Many Stories Told

Scores of curious old stories are told about the abandoned village of Airdrie, and while some of them may have been twisted and distorted in the telling and retelling, the main facts concerning the history of the place are as follows:

Attracted by the lurid word picture of the beauty and wealth of the then sparsely settled state of Kentucky, and by the description of the hilltop upon which the city was started, a company of Scotch capitalists obtained possession of 900 acres of rich land, and on the bluff above the Green River, set out to build a town. Everything went well until modern methods came into competition with those of the Airdrie capitalists. Then came the abandonment of the big tract, General Buell, agent for the corporation, retaining his supervision over the vast estate. He lived there until his death.

When the Scotchmen sent over to build the city arrived on the grounds, they laid the foundation for the old prison about 100 yards from the river banks. Typical of the days before the (Civil) war was the huge bastille they built, three stories high and with walls three feet thick. The stone used in construction of the prison was the best to be found in the state, and today is rare and valuable. The tiers of the cell are dark and damp, the only light filtering in through narrow windows high up in the walls and latticed with iron bars several inches thick.

Down in the ground, under the old prison are more cells, so dark and fetid that a match held above the head flickers for a moment and then is gone, its only mission being to emphasize the blackness of the dungeon. It was in these underground caverns that the unruly prisoners were placed to meditate on their misdeeds, and solitary confinements here must have been well-calculated to break the spirit of the boldest and most obstreperous (sic). Huge iron rings fastened to the solid walls with enormous staples, tell of other disciplinary measures than mere confinement in the dark abyss.

"Prison" Described

At the corner of the prison are located the rooms where the sentinels stood their lonely watches in those by-gone days. The windows of their cabins ran length and breadth of the old pile and lest they slumbered while on duty, it is difficult to see how anyone would be sufficiently daring to attempt an escape from these cells, even were walls not so sheer and high and the iron bars not there to further discourage them..

That they were men desperate enough to take the chances of meeting death at a fall from the walls or from a bullet fired by the ever-watchman guard is a fact, strange as it may seem. It is recounted that on a dark night in midwinter, when a storm wrenched and tore at the cornices of the prison and drove hailstones with the force of bullets with its icy breath, a convict, who on several other occasions had made fruitless attempts to escape, made a rope out of his bed clothing and secured an end to the bars of his cell window and let the other swing free in the wind.

He then in some manner, bent the bars aside sufficiently to allow his body to pass through, seized upon his improvised rope and let himself down to the ground, more than 50 feet below. The storm drowned all sounds and friendly darkness proved an effective cloak for the fleeing prisoner. He was never recaptured, the story goes, although the whole countryside was aroused and guards watched at every avenue of escape.

Other stories, too, are told of efforts to escape from the prison, but they have different endings. In several cases the roar of a sentinel rifle proved sudden death for the unfortunate, and then again a shapeless and mangled heap at the bottom of the wall told the story when the guards made their rounds in the early morning.

The Smelter

Nearby the prison stands the old smelter where part of the convicts labored from early morning until the shadows of evening enveloped the plant. Throughout the night, others worked before the fiery furnaces. Like a silent sentinel stands the old tower now, casting ghostly shadows over the quiet forest; a large cedar tree which has grown and thrived on the topmost pinnacle waves gently in the breeze. In niches of

A view of the inside of the old machine shop, frequently and erroneously called the Airdrie prison.

the walls, ferns and other smaller growth have forced their roots, the accumulated dirt of half a century making fertile ground for their sustenance.

A stone's throw from the prison and smelter is the entrance to the mine. In the tortuous and dark passageways, dozens of cars stand, telling a grim story of neglect and ruin. It was here that hundreds of convicts worked that ceaseless ordeal to get out the coal and the ore that made the existence of the town possible. Under the stern eyes of unrelenting watchmen, these men toiled, paying heavy toll for their offenses.

The Alum Spring

Not far from the mine is an alum spring that has flowed for 50 years. The waters of this spring are famed for their medicinal qualities, and it is said that when mixed with river water, the combination is most pleasing to the palate and also has the virtue of being as clear as crystal. The spring is situated in a little declivity which later broadens into a deep ravine. Over this rent in the earth is a rustic bridge, its dilapidated condition in thorough keeping with the general air of the old village and its timbers harmonizing perfectly with the woodland color scheme.

Beneath the bridge is a cavern that has always been more or less a mystery to the people of the countryside.

Deep in the bowels of the earth are hidden chambers, said to compare favorably in point of beauty with some of those to be found in the Mammoth Cave area. Many parties have explored the passages and rooms, but it is not recorded that anyone ever reached the end of several of the tunnels that stretch out under the ground like the tentacles of a huge octopus.

A story is told of two prisoners who escaped the vigilances of their guards and sought to gain freedom in flight. Closely pursued by the sentinels, it is said they sought refuge in the cavern under the rustic bridge.

Bloodhounds traced them to their hiding place, and heavily armed men stood guard at the entrance to await their return from the black depths. Waiting proved to be a tiresome occupation and a dozen of the bolder guards went into the cave to effect a capture. They carried candles and balls of twine, the latter used to facilitate their return to daylight. Although every corner of the place was searched, no trace of the fugitives was ever found. The entrance was carefully guarded for several weeks, but the men never came out, and it is supposed they either found some undiscovered exit or perished in one of the seemingly endless tunnels.

The Hotel Murder

Possibly none of the tales recounted of happenings in Airdrie in the days of its prosperity are more thrilling, and at the same time, gruesome, than the one told of the murder of a young woman in the old hotel. The truth of this story is well-established, although the details are vague at times in the recounting.

The hotel is a rambling old structure and from the outside gives small indication of being more than an ordinary house, neglected and falling in ruins. Inside, there is a difference. Although the furnishings have long since been removed, the general atmosphere of the place is that of an old-time inn. Leading to the second floor is a rickety old stairway, and the visitor with temerity to risk his neck may ascend to the second floor and see the room where the murder took place. This is a bare and musty place with an indefinable air of mystics which still linger in the dimly lighted interior.

It was here that a young woman, traveling unescorted through stress of circumstances, stopped for the night. It was bitter cold and a roaring fire burned in the big fireplace. The weary traveler, who according to report, was the daughter of a wealthy land owner, had slept only a few hours when two robbers entered the room. The girl was given no chance to make an outcry, being throttled by the larger of the men while she slept. She was subjected to every indignity, according to the tradition, and when showing signs of regaining her senses was killed. Not content with slaying their victim, the murderers cut off her head and threw it into the fire, where it was partly consumed before the burned down embers sank down into the ashes and caused it (the head) to roll out onto the floor and in the morning it was found there. A hole in the flooring, the charred edges and black, still remains to show where the head rested after rolling out of the flames. The body was taken away from the hotel and hidden and, despite a search extending over several weeks was never found. As the young lady wore several valuable pieces of jewelry when last seen, robbery is believed to have been the prime motive for the attack and subsequent murder.

Other stories of midnight orgies in the old hostelry are told and according to tales handed down from generation to generation, gambling for high stakes was a frequent occurrence. In one of the rooms on the first floor, which at one time was used as a card room, there is an old table, its legs fast rotting away and the top scarred with the mistreatment accorded by hands that have long since been consigned to the grave. On the one corner is a dark stain and on the floor another, and it is held by some of the older residents of the vicinity that this is a grim memento of one of the last card games in which one of the players lost his life by reason of his dexterity in manipulating the cards. It is not hard to believe that this story is true, for the stains bear mute evidence of the tragedy enacted in ante-bellum days.

A Paradise for Ghosts

It is not strange that the old pile is said to be haunted and is shunned by all Negroes within many miles, and also by many whites. It is an ideal place for "ghosts" and one would have to go a long way to find a house in which spirits could better disport themselves than here.

Until recently when it was destroyed by fire, the old home of General Buell was one of the chief places of interest in Airdrie. For many years the old fighter lived in the old colonial mansion. He had the place fitted to suit his tastes, and rich tapestries and rare paintings were only a part of the furnishing provided to suit the artistic ideas of General Buell. Here the old man lived with dozens of servants to wait upon him. It is said that he spent most of his time in his study and that this part of the house was zealously guarded from the prying eyes of strangers. General Buell read a great deal and was supposed to have some secret which caused the close guard to be kept on his study. Rumors told of a secret room beneath the house and of hidden stairways in the walls, but their authenticity could never be proven since the old man left orders that after his death the study should be sealed and no one allowed to enter. His orders were strictly obeyed by the servants, and no one ever set foot in there after his death. Before a solution of the mystery attached to the place could be solved by some latter-day investigator, the old mansion was destroyed by fire. Whether or not the flames were started deliberately probably will never be known, but that they leaped to their work of devastation from a dozen different places is an allegation generally credited.

Perhaps in the future some man or men with capital may solve the transportation problems and resurrect Airdrie from the death-like sleep. Until then the little village will continue to be a show place for the infrequent visitor who happens in that direction and a playground for birds and beasts. It is not likely that the hum of machinery will soon shatter the silence that is almost perpetual, but should that ever be, Kentucky will lose one of her most picturesque and beautiful curiosities.

(Author unknown)

Old Airdrie on Green River

By HELEN HENRY
Central City, Kentucky. Times-Argus (1949)

(Note: Helen Henry was a general assignment reporter for the Central City, Kentucky Times-Argus before becoming editor of the Louisville Magazine in 1950.)

The moss-covered, willow-lined banks of Green River hide many secrets of days gone by, and groves of beech and oak shadow many a silent deserted spot which once echoed to the ring of pioneer axes and the shouts of toiling men.

No spot on the length of this winding Western Kentucky stream is more steeped in tradition than the site of Old Airdrie, once a thriving industrial town, now only a ghostly collection of batter brick heaps. Only a few ancient, tottering steps and a few mounds of old stone serve as a reminder of the days, nearly a century ago, when Airdrie was the "Scotland of the West", a center for the mining and smelting of pig iron.

The history of Airdrie does not begin until 1855, but the events leading to its settlement go back into the eighteenth century, before the making of the state. In 1791, surveyors and geologists of Virginia, exploring the County of Kentucky, found deposits of iron ore in the western region. The first iron furnace in Kentucky was the Bourbon furnace built in Bath County before 1800. It was at a furnace in Eddyville that William Kelly in 1851, developed the so-called Bessemer process which revolutionized the steel industry.

During the 1830s the old Buckner furnace, known as "The Stack" was erected. It was built by Aylette Buckner, father of Civil War General Simon Bolivar Buckner. For several years he worked the furnace, situated about five miles south of Greenville in Muhlenberg County.

Airdrie, successor to "The Stack", is located on the river off Kentucky Highway 81 (later US Highway 431) and about 15 miles from the junction with US Highway 62 at Central City and 120 miles southwest of Louisville. *(Editor's note: Perhaps Drakesboro, at the intersection of Highways 431 and 176 would have been a better reference point.)* The town derived its name from a small city in Scotland, between Edinburgh and Glasgow. It was the ancestral home of Sir Robert Sproul Crawford Aitcheson Alexander.. Born in Kentucky, he was educated in Scotland. After succeeding to the title, he returned to America. His supply of Black Band iron ore in Scotland was almost exhausted, and so he searched for a similar ore in this country. His geologists discovered a desirable ore, first near the abandoned Buckner furnace and then near Paradise, at Airdrie. Alexander bought 17,000 acres of land in the county, all except the Buckner property lying along Green River, centered about a mile from Paradise.

Believing that the Scotch were the best ironmongers in the world, Alexander brought many of his former employees and their families to his new Airdrie. A special ship was chartered for the six-week voyage. The Scotsmen landed at New York, journeyed to Pittsburgh and thus down the Ohio River to Louisville. From there they traveled further down the Ohio and up Green River to their "New Scotland."

Alexander spared no expense in the building of his community. He invested more than $350,000 in erecting a furnace, stone house, mill, hotel, a few two-story frame houses and about 25 frame cottages.

The iron works and mines were ranged along a narrow strip of land between the water's edge and the top of a bluff. The massive furnace, over 55 feet high, was built of river sandstone. The stack, which stood until recently, was erected on a square base with Roman arches for the opening under the kiln. The "Stone House", used for machinery, was built a few feet from the furnace. This structure was three stories high, 20 by 50 feet. About halfway up the wall the architect placed the inscription, *"Airdrie, 1855."*

Much of the time was spent digging and drilling, but the furnace was finally started, and the Scotch workers watched happily as the stack belched forth its first crimson flames. Alexander gave his workers full sway in production, and the pig iron of Airdrie Hill was turned out by the same methods used in Scotland.

While the iron workers were familiar with the handling of the Black Band ore of Scotland, they did not realize that the Kentucky ore required a different treatment. Three or four attempts to run the furnace were made, all unsuccessful.

Alexander's patience was exhausted, and he set a date for discontinuing the work. Although drillers discovered new veins of ore on the last day, he (Alexander) refused to continue the work. The settlement was abandoned in 1857, after two years of operation. Alexander retired to his Bluegrass stock farm near Lexington and at the time of his death ten years later, he was reputed to be the richest man in Kentucky.

Sir Robert was a quiet, unassuming man, known to his employees as "The Lord." One story is told of a woodsman named Williams who visited Airdrie and belligerently demanded to see "that thar lord." On seeing Alexander he walked around him, sizing him up. He finally remarked, "So you're th' lord, air ye? By gum, you're nothing but a human bein' after all, and a plain, ordinary, say-little sort of feller at that. They said you was a big bug, but five foot six will reach you any day in the week, by Washington!" The amused "Lord" gave Williams a hearty handshake and a few weeks later the backwoodsman presented "Lord Ellick" with "enough venison for all Scotland."

The later active history of Airdrie is centered about one man — Civil War General Don Carlos Buell. This Union soldier is best known for his rapid march to Louisville from Shiloh in time to prevent the fall of the city to Bragg's forces, and for his success in driving the Confederate army from Kentucky after the battle of Perryville.

General Buell was mustered out of the service in 1864. Two years later he took a 40-year lease for mineral and oil rights on the Airdrie property. He occupied the rambling, many roomed Alexander house for 32 years.

Finding more coal than oil on the property, General Buell concentrated his operations on coal development. He fought through the legislature for 15 years against the unfair freight rate policies of the Green and Barren Rivers Navigation Company which had a lease on Green River. His work resulted in the purchase of the lease by the Federal Government and subsequent improvement of navigation conditions on the river.

Buell died in 1898. In 1908, Airdrie was sold by his heirs to a Central City coal company (Five J), which still (in 1949) owns the property.

Many extravagant tales have been told about Airdrie. The Stone House has sometime been called the Old Prison. Some story tellers maintain that Alexander worked prisoners in his mines; others say that Buell held Civil War prisoners in the three-story structure. The truth is much tamer. Buell used 15 prisoners sent from the state penitentiary for a few weeks to help quarry stone.[5]

---

[5] *Editor's note: These prisoners were actually working*

Ghost stories are the favorite tales of Airdrie. The old hotel, largest building in the community, is the center of the ghost stories. The weather-beaten walls, broken windows, and the generally dilapidated condition gave rise to the report that the hotel was haunted. Most of the stories concern a murder scene in the dark of midnight and the later activities of a headless ghost.

Such is the history of Airdrie. Few traces can now be found of the deserted village. The scores of house have been demolished. The Buell residence burned 40 years ago and even the stone chimneys and foundation have crumbled. Among the cedars and sycamores high on the bluff are the ruins of "The Stack," covered by creeping vines and encroaching bushes. The Stone House has entirely disappeared.[6] Only holes in the ground representing the shafts indicate that mines were once drilled.

The park between the site of the Buell mansion and the river was once one of the most beautifully landscaped spots in Western Kentucky. It is now a jungle. The winding walkways are obscured by ivy and honeysuckle, and the wide lawn is a mass of weeds.

The old Scotch names now scattered through Muhlenberg County — McLean, Hendrie, Alney, Duncan, Alexander, Sumner, Gilmour, Robertson, MacDougal, MacDonald, Southerland, Bruce, Torrence — these are the

---

for the state, while they were quarrying stone for the new prison at Eddyville and were under state supervision.. The task at Airdrie was short-lived. The state found a source of stone nearer to Eddyville.

[6] Editor's note: This is in error. The Stack was never atop the bluff but still stands on the river level below the bluff line. Today, in the year 2000, it remains remarkably well-preserved, 145 years after it was erected..

heritage of Airdrie. This strange, short-lived community is now a ghost town. Only the endless flow of the green waters of the river is the same as in the day of "New Airdrie."

Airdrie and Muhlenberg

By JOE CREASON

Louisville, Kentucky, Courier-Journal

(Circa 1961)

Muhlenberg County is a 472 square mile plot of rolling mineral-rich real estate in west central Kentucky that would be unusual among Kentuckiana counties if only because:

1. It is bounded on three sides by three different rivers.

2. It can lay claim to having one small corner that is absolute Paradise.

3. It is the location of perhaps the only rock ever formally dedicated to a hillbilly-type song.

These three distinctions, dissimilar as they are, really meld into and are a part of the Muhlenberg County story.

The county, No. 34 among Kentucky's 120 in order of establishment, is bordered on the west by Pond River, on the most of its north by Green River and on the east by Mud River; one of the county's oldest towns has the real and legal name of Paradise and is now the site of the world's largest steam-electric power plants; seven years ago county residents raised money to place a one-ton rock near the town of Ebenezer in honor of the song *"Sixteen Tons,"* an all-time hit written by native son Merle Travis.

On November 30, Merle Travis Day was celebrated at Greenville, the county seat, honoring this home-town boy who made good in the country music field.

Actually, Muhlenberg County doesn't have to rely upon natural, name or man-made oddities to stand out. Its rich history, its present standing as a leading coal-producing county and its future potential — once the impact of the 1,300,000-kilowatts of power to be produced at the

Paradise steam plant has been felt — give it a flavor and color not equaled by many Kentucky or Indiana counties.

Settled first in 1795 and named for General John Peter Gabriel Muhlenberg, it is rich in history that is spiced by the likes of the villainous Harp brothers, early coal miners, Jesse James, Scotch iron makers, Civil War generals and many other romantic figures.

The county was formed formally in 1798 and Greenville, near to where the first settlement was made at Caney Station, was selected as the seat of government.

Early in the 1800s the Harp brothers, who had left a bloody trail across Kentucky, reached the middle Green River country. Local tradition holds that the outlaws were pursued and that Micajah, oldest of the pair, was mortally wounded and captured on a hill back from Pond River, west of the present town of Graham. His head was severed from his body and carried to the nearest magistrate, in what is now Webster County and there placed in the fork of a tree (beside the road).

The place where Harp was captured is still known as Harp's Hill.[7]

It wasn't until 1820 or thereabouts that "black rock" (coal) was first mined near Stum's Landing, now Paradise, and sent by barge down the Green River to Evansville and Owensboro.

However, wood was so plentiful and convenient that little attention was paid to the rich coal deposits. Not until the early 1850s when Dr. David Owen, then America's leading geologist, studied and reported on the great

---

[7] *The Harp brothers were also known to have resided for a while on Harp's Hill, in a natural rock formation known today as "Harp's House."*

deposits in Muhlenberg County did mining begin in earnest.

One thing that spurred the industry was the attempt at Airdrie, a Scotch-founded community near Paradise, to use coal in refining the surface iron ore found in the area without (first) converting it to coke.

Prior to that, an iron furnace had been erected in 1837 in the southern part of the county by the father of Simon Bolivar Buckner, Civil War Confederate general and later governor of Kentucky. It had used charcoal exclusively in working the surface iron center.

Meanwhile, at the same time the Buckner and Airdrie furnaces were in operation, coal was being mined elsewhere in the county in limited quantities.

It was at one of the coal operations (Dovey) that Jesse James paid his visit to the county in 1881. Late in the summer, a stoop-shouldered stranger appeared at the mine near Mercer, at the time operated by John Dovey and his two sons, and asked for work. In the course of the conversation, Dovey remarked that next day was pay day at the mine.

Next morning, after the miners had gone underground, three men, one of them the stranger from the day before, walked into the office and demanded all of the money on hand. Fortunately one of the sons had gone into town for the payroll and had not returned, so only $13 was taken from the safe.

Later it was definitely established that the stoop-shouldered leader of the bandits was Jesse James.

For more than 60 years Muhlenberg has been one of Kentucky's leading coal producers. Present output runs more than 10,000,000 tons per year, most of it by the strip or surface mining method. The Paradise steam plant, built by the Tennessee Valley Authority, has boosted production substantially.

Incidentally, Peabody Coal Company, which is supplying coal for the monster plant, has assembled the world's largest self-propelled machine to remove over-burden from coal to be mined. This shovel weighs 18,000,000 pounds and is as tall as a 20-story building.

As to topography, the surface of Muhlenberg County generally is rolling, with good farming land occurring in the south portion mainly. The 1960 population was about 28,000, down considerably from the 1950 figures, due to continued mechanization in mining.

Points of Interest

The author listed these points of interest to be seen in Muhlenberg County.

1. Harp's Hill, near Graham, where the famous outlaw, Big Harp, was captured and slain.

2. Bremen, which wears the name of the Old World seaport town of the German settlers which founded it.

3. South Carrollton, an old Green River town, once the site of the South Carrollton Male and Female Institute.

4. Central City, the county's largest town, first called Morehead's Horse Mill, later Owensborough Junction and Stroud City and then by its present name.

5. Dovey Mine, southwest of Central City and the mine that Jesse James robbed in 1881.

6. Greenville, the town selected in 1799 as the county seat.

7. "Sixteen Tons" Marker, a short distance off Highway 176, at Ebenezer and west of Drakesboro, dedicated in 1956 to Merle Travis and the song by the same name.

8. Airdrie, where the ruins of the Airdrie furnace are to be found. It was once a booming iron ore smelting town, established in 1855.

9. Paradise, the tiny village and one of the county's first river ports, dwarfed by the immense TVA steam-electric power plant on Green River.

10. Buckner Stack, a pile of rocks remains as a reminder of this furnace which smelted iron ore in the 1830s and had a stack 80 feet in height.

11. Lake Malone State Park, located near Dunmor around Rocky Creek's Lake Malone. It is an 826 acre state park along the county's south border.

Airdrie Furnace Built in 1855

By Sir R. S. C. A. Alexander

By HOMER ALLEY
Evansville, Indiana Press, December, 1966

Now it is just a wind-swept hilltop, about a mile from Paradise, Ky., but once, it had stores, more than a score of houses, and even a hotel.

Today, not a trace of the town remains.

The town was Airdrie, in Muhlenberg County.

However, the ruins of Airdrie furnace remains remarkably well preserved.

This ruin, which looks as if it might stand forever, is a monument to a town that was — and to a dream that was.

In a valley below the bluff where the town was is the stack of a giant iron furnace, a three-story building to house machinery and a long flight of steps.

This is all that remains of a mammoth enterprise that failed.

Airdrie was built in 1855 by Sir R. S. C. A. Alexander, who invested more than a third of a million dollars in the undertaking before calling it quits. That's a fortune today and an unbelievable amount of money 110 years ago.

The Airdrie operation involved some 17,000 acres in Muhlenberg County. Sir Alexander named the furnace and town after Airdrie, Scotland, which lies about midway between Edinburgh and Glasgow and was the seat of his estate.

Sir Alexander, known as Lord Alexander, was born in Frankfort, Ky., in 1819, but returned to Scotland to become heir to land, a fortune and a title.

Dwindling iron ore reserves in Scotland caused Sir Alexander to look about for a new source of supply. He settled

145

upon the ore found in the Green River area as the best possible substitute.

Sir R. S. C. A. Alexander (whose whole name was Robert Sproul Crawford Aitcheson Alexander) bought 17,000 acres in Muhlenberg County to start operations.

From Scotland he brought masons, carpenters, miners, metal workers, furnace tenders — and a town and industry was built in 1855.

Airdrie's days of ascent were numbered. The work of the masons was sound, but the industrial plans of Sir Alexander were not.

Alexander had calculated to use the coal raw in the furnace, instead of first converting it to coke. The result, according to history, was a product low in quality and short in quantity. Shortly after the furnace began operation, a flywheel broke, forcing a shutdown. This was repaired but there was another mechanical breakdown.

After the second breakdown, Sir Alexander lost his patience and gave up. The furnace was never charged again. The superintendent of the furnace had already made plans to switch to coke, but these plans were never carried out.

In all, the furnace was not in blast more than six weeks to two months.

The men were discharged and the furnace was closed. While this was the end of the industry, the community continued.

The Scots brought here by Sir Alexander brought with them new blood to Muhlenberg County. Many of the names survive and are now an inextricable part of Western Kentucky heritage.

Airdrie is famous for another reason. After the Civil War, Don Carlos Buell, the Union Army general who saved General Grant from defeat at Shiloh, retired to Airdrie.

It was at the Alexander house that Buell wrote his articles about the Civil War.

Today, Airdrie furnace is almost impossible to find by road and not even easy to locate by going down stream on the Green River.

Vegetation has made creeping but inevitable progress in obliterating the traces of man except for the stone work erected by the Scots. Portions of the Airdrie works appear as stable as the day they were built more than 110 years ago. However, ghost stories about Airdrie still persist. There are stories that Alexander used slaves, that Buell held captured Confederate prisoners there and, that it once was a prison.

There's only a kernel of truth in all this. When the State Penitentiary at Eddyville was being enlarged in the early 1880s, a few of the Alexander title and convicts were brought to Airdrie to quarry stone. They were kept at the furnace works.

While the ghost stories probably are without foundation, most any visitor there will tell you that you can stand on top of that hill and almost feel the pulse of the town that once lived.

In a book published in Evansville in 1898 and titled *"The Green River Country,"* this is what is said about Airdrie:

"This is one of the most interesting spots on Green River, not because of any particular charm arising from the natural location or artificial embellishment, but because it is and has been for many years the home of one of America's most illustrious citizens."

The RePrint of *Airdrie*

In 2001, I received a copy of Bobby Anderson's book, Airdrie, which I studied extensively for my fiction novel about the town, *A Mile Below Paradise, Lost City of Airdrie.*

In 2010, I met with the author, who surprised me when he told me he was finished with the Airdrie manuscript. I tried encouraging him to print it again, but he said he was finished and would not do anything more with the book.

I told him I would design a fresh full-color cover and help him, but he said no. I was aghast. He stunned me when he said, "I'm finished with it, but I will give it to you."

I stared at him and had no idea what he meant until I received a package in the mail a few days after the meeting. I was very surprised, excited, and honored to find his files on floppy discs, his hard copies, and instructions in a first-class USPS package.

While I was eager to get to work on a fresh cover and updates, his stipulations sort of took the wind out of my sails. He gave me strict guidelines the younger me did not want to abide by.

I put the project to the side. He did not care; he said he didn't care if I never did anything with it. I put the package in a safe place, always intending to return to the precious project.

It was late in 2023 that I finally decided to do what I had promised. Bobby had passed away years earlier, and I didn't know if he had told anyone about what he had done.

I contacted Bobby's family to ensure they were comfortable with the re-publication. The first response was surprise. His daughter-in-law, Margaret, told me they had searched for his book records, but his computer had been wiped clean of Airdrie, and there was no printed manuscript. I explained why it was missing and texted them the photos of what I had.

To my delight, the family graciously entrusted me with what Bobby had trusted me to do. Their blessing was the shot in the arm I needed to go full throttle and prove I could get the book in print again.

I have published the re-print of Airdrie, abiding by the author's original requests and format preferences as best I could while updating the manuscript for modern sizing issues.

I hope each reader will be as excited as I was to comb the pages and learn the truth about the old city. My original copy is covered with highlighter markings and notes.

I am sure I will be asked why Bobby Anderson trusted me with his work. I wish I had a great answer, but I do not know. I certainly did not deserve the gift. We only met twice, but I really do love this book and its subject. It is my hope that I have honored both Bobby Anderson and his family by preserving the collection he called, *Airdrie*.

Made in the USA
Columbia, SC
13 May 2024